WRITING CLEARLY:
A CONTEMPORARY APPROACH

Edward P. Bailey, Jr.

Charles E. Merrill Publishing Company
A Bell & Howell Company
Columbus   Toronto   London   Sydney

Published by Charles E. Merrill Publishing Company
A Bell & Howell Company
Columbus, Ohio 43216

This book was set in Zapf.

ISBN: 0-675-20269-8

Library of Congress Catalog Card Number: 83-063120

1 2 3 4 5——88 87 86 85 84

Printed in the United States of America

Acknowledgments

Acknowledgments and copyrights continue at the back of the book on page 145, which constitutes an extension of the copyright page.

John R. Trimble, WRITING WITH STYLE: *Conversations on the Art of Writing*, © 1975, pp. 84, 85. Reprinted by permission of Prentice-Hall, Inc., Englewood Cliffs, N.J.

"Our Language, Right or Wrong," Bob Levey's Washington column, *The Washington Post*, Sept. 6, 1982, p. D 17. Reprinted by permission of *The Washington Post*.

Nancy Martin, et al., *Writing and Learning Across the Curriculum*, © 1975, pp. 29, 61, 104–5. Reprinted by permission of Boynton/Book Publishers.

Donald J. Foss, David T. Hakes, *Psycholinguistics: An Introduction to the Psychology of Language* © 1978, p. 326. Reprinted by permission of Prentice-Hall, Inc., Englewood Cliffs, N.J.

List, "The Seven Ground Rules" (pp.11–12) and excerpts, passim (pp. 11, 16, 17, 21, 64), from *Say What You Mean* by Rudolf Flesch. Copyright © 1972 by Rudolf Flesch. Reprinted by permission of Harper & Row, Publishers, Inc.

For my good friends
Janet Hiller, Paul Diehl, Tom Murawski, and Minter Alexander
who inspired this book

CONTENTS

PREFACE

By the time we reach college, I think most of us have run across
—and probably all too often—writing that is so difficult to read
that we just don't want to make the mental effort. Sometimes we
don't have the right background to understand it, sometimes it's
the kind of material that we need to study instead of simply read,
but usually it's just badly written. The term for such stuff is "gobbledygook."

This book examines gobbledygook and recommends specific
ways to avoid writing it.

In the past, books on clear writing had no underlying theory
about what made writing easy or hard; they depended almost
solely on intuition: passive voice *seems* to make sentences harder
to understand; big words *seem* to be harder to understand; and so
forth. But thanks to a recent revolution in the study of reading, we
no longer need to rely only on our intuitions; we can be more empirical by examining the results of some fascinating psychological
experiments.

This book, then, tries to bring the field of clear writing up to
date by applying to it the recent breakthroughs in reading theory.
The results? The traditional books were on the right track, of
course, but their specific advice needs modification in almost
every instance. And in some instances, their advice was, in fact,
wrong.

Yet the book's purpose is more than simply an examination of clear writing, because it applies the new thinking not only in how we read, but also in how we write. I try to show that the style that produces the clearest writing—the informal style—is also easier to write: it allows people to develop a writing personality, or "voice," that helps unblock that channel from the mind to the pen. An informal style thus helps the writing process, promoting the kind of invention, the kind of creativity, that is essential to all kinds of writing, from technical reports to business letters to novels and poems.

I believe this book will be useful in many college writing courses: advanced composition, technical writing, business writing, theory of composition, and even perhaps freshman English. It is not aimed at any particular kind of student, nor, in fact, specifically at students at all. As I wrote the book, I thought of myself as talking to any educated person interested in writing. I hope that anyone, college level or beyond, will find it of value.

A number of people have been very helpful to me in this project.

Professors Paul Diehl and Cathy Wilson, both from the University of Iowa, not only encouraged me from the beginning of this project, but also read the manuscript closely and gave me *invaluable* advice. I am deeply indebted to them for their time and insight. I am also fortunate to have had the assistance of Professors Richard Lloyd-Jones, Robert Wachal, Brooks Landon, and John Harper, also from the University of Iowa.

Professor Tom Murawski, from the U.S. Air Force Academy, really got me interested in clear writing in the first place. He's the creator, in effect, of the Academy's Executive Writing Course that brings the good word to thousands and thousands of military writers each year. Tom's enthusiasm about clear writing—and his energy and expertise—were (and still are) contagious.

Minter Alexander, a colleague of mine when I worked in the Pentagon, was also a strong supporter. We spent hours and hours discussing the nature of clear writing, and as you may guess, we had occasional examples of unclear writing to help with our analysis.

Reviewers who offered helpful comments during the final stages of this manuscript also have my grateful acknowledgment: John Ferre, Karen Pelz, Western Kentucky University; Jan Swearingen, University of Arizona; and Bernice Werner Dicks, Southwestern at Memphis.

Beverly Kolz, my editor at Charles E. Merrill, was always a great help, and our discussions guided me to some important revisions of a conceptual nature. I am grateful for her insight—and, of course, for her support throughout.

Finally, Janet Hiller, at the time an analyst in Washington, D.C., read my manuscript with perceptiveness and care. Believe me, I listened carefully to everything she said. She's my wife, and I offer my special thanks to her.

A   A New Perspective

1 INTRODUCTION

I'm sure you've seen gobbledygook before. If you work in the government bureaucracy, if you work in the military, if you work in business, or if you work—or are a student—in academia, you have surely seen lots of it, too much of it, more than you ever care to see again. In fact, you may even have written some of it. I admit that I have.

Gobbledygook is the affectionate name for that pompous, formal sounding, official sort of language that we usually have trouble understanding. It can intimidate us. When we don't understand it, we may begin to question our abilities as readers, our attention spans, our fitness for our jobs, our general intelligence, and our overall worthiness to be human beings.

Why does gobbledygook have this effect? I think the unspoken argument goes something ike this: "I'm writing this stuff. I know what I mean. If I'm smart enough to write it and you're not smart enough to read it, then I'm smarter than you are." The logic is simple.

Perhaps you have even asked the originator of some gobbledygook a question about what he had written, only to have him point out the answer, right there in black and white, in the middle of his report. At such times, you can really begin to question your abilities.

Let me reassure you, however, that the problem isn't you. The problem is him (or even her). He's the emperor without any clothes.

GOBBLEDYGOOK

I don't know whether or not you are a writer of gobbledygook. When I was, I certainly didn't admit it, especially to myself. But if you'd like to find out about some of the contemporary ideas on how to write more clearly and more easily, then this book is designed for you. Before I explain my approach, however, let's look at some examples of gobbledygook. Then you will see the kind of writing I do not consider good

I'll keep the examples of gobbledygook fairly short, but, even so, don't feel obligated to read them all the way through. Just skim them.

From Government Writing

I'll start with government writing, because it has the worst reputation. The following is an excerpt from the *Federal Register*. The excerpt is a summary of the more detailed material following it. You would think that a summary would be especially readable:

> *SUMMARY:* This amends the Commission's independent ocean freight forwarder regulations to remove restrictions against affiliations between such forwarders and persons who have a beneficial interest in export shipments via oceangoing common carriers. These revisions are necessary to conform the regulations to amendments to the Shipping Act, 1916, made by the Omnibus Budget Reconciliation Act of 1981.[1]

This example isn't impossible to understand, but if you're like me, you had to read it fairly slowly and probably reread a few phrases. A good writer doesn't make you reread just to figure out what he's saying.

From Military Writing

In this one, notice that many of the words, starting with the second sentence, come in batches of "(modifier) (modifier) noun" or even "(modifier) (modifier) (modifier) noun." Reformers of writing in the military call them "hut-two-three-four phrases."

> There are a variety of standards the Army utilizes for classifying an item for repair.
> Aircraft components and assemblies are scheduled for overhaul based on forecast requirements computed from projected aircraft inventory, flying hour programs, and adjusted mean time to removal. The latter is the average operational time between removal, whether premature or allowable time-between-overhaul. Time-between-overhaul is the maximum allowable operating time (expressd in hours) after which it is mandatory that the component be removed from the aircraft for overhaul. Airframe overhaul requirements are based upon reliability centered maintenance strategies wherein the need for depot overhaul is determined by the actual inspection of each aircraft plus estimates of aircraft requiring overhaul as a result of crash damages.
> Missile overhaul requirements are also based upon reliability centered maintenance strategies. Missile system end items of ground equipment are overhauled primarily on the basis of hours of operations....[2]

Writing doesn't get much worse. Actually, you may be surprised to learn that this excerpt was not intended to be writing. It was intended to be speaking—testimony before Congress. Quick thinking Congressmen can usually succeed in getting such testimony published in the record without having to listen to it. You can certainly understand why.

From Business Writing

I've chosen an example of business writing intended for the general public: an advertisement for, I think, prefabricated buildings. Notice that the sentences don't seem to be connected to each other. You can almost see the writer thinking, writing a sentence, and then stopping; thinking, writing another sentence, and stopping; thinking, writing.... He seems to be producing writing that's in individual sentences instead of in paragraphs or larger blocks of thought. The advertisement seems built of parts that either don't go together or weren't put together.

> Growing businesses must expand their facilities to accommodate new inventory and increased production. Such growth in today's highly competitive market comes through a well-planned expansion program. Buildings can constitute the bulk of a business investment and are the basis for successful expansion programs. Proper planning of details during the building purchase can assure correct allocation of capital, scheduled occupancy and a quicker return on the business investment along with minimum operating expense. . . .[3]

From Academic Writing

Yes, bad writing is also entrenched in colleges and universities. The excerpt below is the first three sentences from an article about, ironically, how our brains "process" words as we listen or read.

> Psycholinguistic activity is, essentially, the collocation of many information processing routines which occur when utterances are produced and understood. A major goal of psycholinguistic theory, therefore, is to characterize the information activated and operated upon at various levels of the comprehension process. The experiments reported here were concerned primarily with the retrieval and use of the semantic information associated with individual lexical items in ambiguous sentential contexts.[4]

The Problem with Gobbledygook

You can see that gobbledygook has little allegiance to any one profession, thus the other names it has acquired: "bureaucratese," "governmentese," "militarese," "businessese," "legalese," and "academese." Regardless of its name, however, it is basically the same sort of bad writing.

You may have noticed that some of the passages of gobbledygook I quoted made sense to you. Doesn't that mean that they aren't really gobbledygook? If you could read them at an easy pace and understand them with no especial difficulty, then I'd have to say that they aren't. But I doubt if you could do that.

Most writing is to be read, not studied. So if you find yourself constantly re-reading words, even if you can eventually see that they make sense, even if you can finally re-read a passage with little effort after spending some time with it, you're probably reading gobbledygook. There's seldom any reason for a writer to make you struggle through his work.

In an excellent book called *The Language of the Law*, David Mellinkoff makes the same point. He then quotes from Oliver Wendell Holmes, a former Associate Justice on the U.S. Supreme Court, who used the following simple and lively language to distinguish between a wrong that is intentional and one that is caused by negligence: ". . . even a dog distinguishes between being stumbled over and being kicked."[5]

Holmes's brilliance we can only hope for; his clarity we can—and should—achieve.

THE ALTERNATIVE

This book probably won't do much good for the gobbledygook writers I have just quoted, and you probably don't think that you belong in their category. But most people, including most of those I ran into during three years in Washington, D.C., could write much more clearly than they do. By learning a relatively few new writing techniques, you could make your writing much more readable than it probably is right now. However, I know from experience—not just as a teacher of writing, but also as a writer—that to apply those techniques, you also need a new way of thinking, not just about commas and semicolons, but about writing, about yourself as a writer, and about your readers. That requires a conceptual breakthrough.

In the first part of this book, Chapters 1-4, I will tell you the discoveries that helped me make my own conceptual breakthrough. Then in the second part of this book, Chapters 5 through 11, I will explain some specific skills that you can use to make your writing easier to read.

But is easiness on the reader what you're after? Most people think that if only they knew a few more rules on how to use a comma, or if only they could remember whether "per cent" or "percent" was correct, or if only they had paid more attention in their English course 5 or 50 years ago, then they could be good writers.

Well, good writing is not just following all of the rules, or knowing more rules and better ones. Once you're fairly competent with the basics of writing—you don't misspell too many words, you know how to put subjects and verbs together, you start with capital letters and end with periods—then you probably don't need more rules. In fact, most experts in writing would no doubt tell you that you know too many rules already, that the rules get in your way, and that the ones you're afraid you don't know may get in your way even more. What you need, then, is not more rules but a new approach, the one all good professional writers have whether they know it or not, and most of them do know it.

LEARNING HOW TO WRITE

Six or seven years ago, I decided that I knew enough about teaching college English—I had taught for five years—to write a textbook. I really felt that I had developed an approach worth putting in a book, but somehow I couldn't get started. I looked on my shelves at some of the other writing textbooks, hoping for a hint on how to begin.

I made several attempts, some as many as three or four pages long. The writing was really hard work. I tried and tried. The words I wrote sounded like textbook writing, I thought, the kind a publisher might buy, but each word came only after great effort. Finally, I gave up.

Almost exactly a year later, I tried again, with the same result. Then I had my inspiration. I told myself, "I've had it with this nonsense. First I'll just write things down the way I say them to my class. Then I'll convert that writing into something 'publishable.'"

So I imagined myself in class, sitting on the edge of my desk and talking to the students in front of me. As I visualized the scene, I wrote the words I thought I would say to them. In one of the great surprises of my life, the words came easily, as though I had just removed some sort of blockage. I wrote the first chapter with little problem.

Occasionally the old habits would intervene, so I'd just remind myself of the scene that had gotten me started—sitting on my desk and talking to the class—and I'd find the style that worked again.

Well before I finished the book, I knew that I wasn't about to convert my writing to "textbookese." And I didn't need to, for the publisher bought the book immediately, and a second book two years later. Afterward, in talking with my editor, I found out that if I had persevered somehow in the traditional, textbook style, I probably wouldn't have sold the book at all. She said that she rejects many manuscripts a year for that very reason. And if you look around at recent books, at least in the field of English, you will see that most are written in the new, clearer style.

What had I learned from my experience? I had learned how to write so that the words would come far more easily than they ever had before. And, as a side benefit, I had learned to write clearly.

In a way, I'm coming at things from a different direction in this book. I'm going to offer advice to you on how to write clearly. *But the style I describe for clear writing has the immense advantage of also helping you get your words and ideas on paper much more easily.* Not all the time—not, for example, if you don't know your facts or if you don't have the right background for whatever you're writing—but that's not a problem of writing, is it? In other cases, though, this new style will help.

A NEW PERSPECTIVE

As I mentioned, this book is in two parts: Part A, "A New Perspective"; and Part B, "A New Style." The first part is important background for the second part, which offers specific advice on just how to write more clearly and more easily.

Let me give you a brief overview of each part. Part A, "A New Perspective," brings you up to date on some contemporary views of language, writing, and reading. I have a chapter on each.

In the chapter on language, I'll try to expose some misconceptions—often purveyed as the gospel by the "pop grammarians"—that do serious damage to the writing process. Is most writing good? Does some writing have to be difficult in order

to be precise? Can you improve your writing by paying more attention to the rules? I'll deal with these and other questions.

In the next chapter in Part A, I'll discuss the writing process. If
you remember learning in school that you should make a complete outline before you begin writing, or that every paragraph
should have a topic sentence, then you're in for some pleasant surprises. The contemporary approach lifts such burdens rather than
imposes them—and it contains the answer to why I couldn't write
that textbook when I tried to adopt an unnatural style.

Finally in Part A, I have a chapter on how we read. Several
years ago, there didn't seem to be much connection between the
study of writing and the study of reading. But think about it for a
minute. If you believe, as I do, that clear writing is writing that is
easy to read, then shouldn't we consider just what kind of writing
is, in fact, easy on the reader? During the past decade or so, there
have been some important breakthroughs in reading theory—
revolutionary breakthroughs that I find fascinating and exciting—
that now permit us to examine more empirically the question of
readability. In this chapter I'll present a model of how we read,
complete with summaries of some interesting psychological experiments that help explain it. This chapter, then, lays important
groundwork for the next part of the book.

Next, Part B, "A New Style," relies heavily on the new science
of reading in giving specific recommendations on how you should
write. Should you really use short words? Should you write short
sentences? Is there any reason to avoid the passive voice? What
about abbreviations, acronyms, jargon, concrete words, question
marks, dashes, prepositions at the ends of sentences? We don't
have to rely on our intuition any longer. With the new science of
reading, we can often test our intuition with empirical studies. In
some cases, our intuition was right. In others. . . .

And I'll back up my advice, not just with assertions from reading theory, but by telling you about the experiments behind them.

I hope you find this approach as exciting as I do.

A NEW STYLE

You're probably wondering, at this point, just what style I am going
to recommend in Part B. At its most general level, my advice isn't

much different from what the traditional books on clear writing have been giving for years: write more informally, write the way you talk (unless you've learned how to talk gobbledygook), use simpler words. But the more specific advice—the advice on how, exactly, to write more informally, etc.—is quite new. The advances in reading theory have seen to that.

In case you're worried, your style need not be quite as informal and personal as I'm using in this book; unfortunately, not every occasion will permit that. But with the techniques I will show you, you can make your style as personal as this one or as formal as you like (you just won't like an extra-formal style any longer). The new approach is very versatile.

A FINAL NOTE

My boss, when I worked in Washington, became an avid convert to the new, clearer style of writing. One day as he was writing a report that we considered quite important, he said, "You know, I'm sure there's a time you couldn't use this style of writing. I'm sure there is. But I just can't seem to think of one."

Frankly, I can't either.

Notes for Chapter 1

1. 46 CFR Part 510, "Licensing of Independent Ocean Freight Forwarders," Federal Maritime Commission, *Federal Register* ("Rules and Regulations"), 47, No. 109 (June 7, 1982), 24555.

2. U.S. Congress, House Appropriations Committee, *DOD Appropriations for 1978: Part I, Budget Hearings*, 95th Congress (Washington, D.C.: GPO, 1977), pp. 277-78.

3. Advertisement for Morton Buildings, *Business and Industry Magazine*, April 1982, p. 26.

4. Helen S. Cairns and Joan Kamerman, "Lexical Information Processing During Sentence Comprehension," *Journal of Verbal Learning and Verbal Behavior*, 14 (1975), 170.

5. Oliver Wendell Holmes, *The Common Law 3* (1881), in *The Language of the Law* by David Mellinkoff (Boston: Little, Brown, 1963), p. 29.

2 SOME CRUCIAL MISCONCEPTIONS

It must be clear to you already that this book urges a simpler, more natural style of writing for two reasons: such a style is easier for your reader to understand, and it is also easier for you to write. Why then, you may ask, do people ever begin writing gobbledygook?

Some people think gobbledygook writers are unclear on purpose, hoping to tire or confuse their readers into giving up. That is occasionally true, perhaps, but not very often. First, most of the bureaucratic writers I know would be shocked to find out they are writing gobbledygook—after all, *they* know what they mean. Second, they are almost always trying to write as well as they can. If they want to be, shall we say, a bit Machiavellian, it is by hoping people *will* understand and believe what they say—contorted statistics, misdirections, omissions, ambiguities, whatever. It is not by having the readers simply give up in frustration. Lastly, internal memos, exchanged among the friendlies, are as notoriously unreadable as the letters and reports for outsiders.

The causes for gobbledygook, then, must lie elsewhere.

SOME CAUSES OF GOBBLEDYGOOK

I just said that most writers usually try to write as well as they can. Unfortunately, they have a number of misconceptions about writing that cause them to write badly even though they try to write well. These misconceptions make writers so concerned with being "correct," with coming across as intelligent and educated people, that their writing process is seriously disturbed. That's what happened to me when I tried to write my first book in a "publishable" style.

One result of excessive and usually needless concern with correctness is that the writer's words and ideas flow only very slowly, as though they have to push past some sort of blockage. I will explain this further in the next chapter on the writing process. The other result is that the writing becomes overly formal and difficult to read.

For the rest of the chapter, then, I will cover some of the common misconceptions about writing and language that make people afraid to express themselves naturally. At one point or another in my adult life, I have held all of these misconceptions.

Misconception: Most Writing Is Good

When people read something and have trouble understanding it, they often unselfishly take the blame themselves. In a popular college textbook called *A Contemporary Rhetoric,* Maxine Hairston makes the same point quite clearly:

> . . . students do not think of the writing in . . . magazines as appropriate models for class papers. Actually, it often is.
>
> What many students do seem to see as appropriate models for their own college papers is the kind of writing that they sometimes encounter in textbooks, literary criticism, and professional journals. While much, perhaps most, of the writing from these sources is clear and instructive [I think Hairston is being polite here], unfortunately some of it is also unclear and unnecessarily pedantic and wordy. Moreover, often it is just the article that students are having the most trouble with that they think is the most scholarly and impressive. Ironically, inexperienced readers almost never say to themselves, "I am having a hard time reading this book or article because it is

badly written." Rather they say, "I am having a hard time reading this because I am stupid. And the author must be saying
something very important because I don't understand many
of the big words and expressions."[1]

Hairston then presents excerpts from two textbooks and tells
the students that the writing in them is much more difficult than it
need be. According to her, the content of those books is "important
in spite of, not because of, the style."[2]

Let me give my own example. One book well known for its
content is Thomas Kuhn's *The Structure of Scientific Revolutions.*
Kuhn shows that revolutionary scientific discoveries don't just add
to our knowledge but require us to change our perspective on
what we had accepted before. I think the book is a brilliant one,
but it is also quite hard to read. Here, for example, are the book's
first three sentences:

> History, if viewed as a repository for more than anecdote or
> chronology, could produce a decisive transformation in the
> image of science by which we are now possessed. That image
> has previously been drawn, even by scientists themselves,
> mainly from the study of finished scientific achievements as
> these are recorded in the classics and, more recently, in the
> textbooks from which each new scientific generation learns to
> practice its trade. Inevitably, however, the aim of such books is
> persuasive and pedagogic; a concept of science drawn from
> them is no more likely to fit the enterprise that produced them
> than an image of national culture drawn from a tourist bro-
> chure or a language text.[3]

Does that excerpt make sense? Yes (especially now that I've read
the rest of the book). Is it easy reading? No.

The point, then, is that you should not assume that most of
what you read is a good model for you to follow. Just because
something is published, or just because it has a signature at the
bottom of it, or just because that's the way most people write,
doesn't mean that that's what you should do.

Can all of those people—the ones who make reading so hard
—really be wrong? After all, there are many of them and only one
of you. I remember recently observing college students taking a
ballroom dance class. They knew they were all supposed to dance

in either a clockwise or a counter-clockwise direction, but they couldn't remember which one. Instead of asking their instructor, they looked sheepishly around and then started moving in a clockwise direction—about thirty of them, all moving the wrong way. Nobody had spoken, nobody had admitted ignorance, yet there they were—all of them wrong.

Misconception: Language Has an Ideal Form

Who do you think the experts on language are today? Edwin Newman? John Simon? William Zinsser? Those are undoubtedly the names that Newman, Simon, and Zinsser would give, but they would be wrong.

Perhaps you have read one of Edwin Newman's books, such as *Strictly Speaking: Will America Be the Death of English?* Newman makes a great outcry that the language is declining, that through carelessness and stupidity, people are departing farther and farther from good English. The result, he feels, is that true communication between people is being hindered—even prevented.

If you've read Newman, you also know that his favorite method is to quote a "slip" and then to ridicule whoever made it. Here's a sample of Newman's wit as he takes on the *New York Times:*

> ... While the motto of the *Times,* "All the News That's Fit to Print," is not exactly shy and retiring, it is not the news in the *Times* I mean to have at. It is the English. The English is not always fit to print. Far from it.
>
> For long years now, one of the worst things the *Times* has done is to use the construction "convince to." You may convince that. You may convince of. You may not convince to. Unfortunately, this use has caught on and is now virtually accepted. ...
>
> Here is an editorial in which the *Times* remarks that the Soviet Union "evidently is not able to convince Cairo to accept a rapid cease-fire."[4]

First, I can't help wondering what system of values a person has who thinks "one of the worst things the *Times* has done is to use the construction 'convince to.'" And frankly, the use of "convince to" in Newman's sample sounds fine to me.

But the point is not whether Newman is right on a matter of usage. The point is that he has no authority for his pronouncements on usage. Yet he seems to have a "Good Book" somewhere, or a stone tablet, where all of his rules are written down. But he doesn't. And there's no such thing.

What about a dictionary? Not really. For at least the past couple of decades, dictionary writers—called "lexicographers"—have seen themselves as historians rather than as lawmakers.[5] That is, their goal is to record the language as it *is* spoken and written, not as it *should be* spoken and written. Why? Most lexicographers and linguists today believe that the standard for correctness should be how people actually use the language. A dictionary, then, is more like a history book of the very recent past—depending on the date of the dictionary—than a permanent book of rules for spelling, meaning, and usage.

Of course we should consult a dictionary when we have a question, but we should realize that since the language changes constantly, dictionaries must change, too, to reflect the way people actually use the language. Yet Newman seems to believe in an authority other than what people like you and me consider acceptable: "Unfortunately, this use [of "convince to"] has caught on and is now virtually accepted." Why does Newman say "unfortunately"?

He doesn't seem to have a standard for his objection. What if he had objected to the increasing synonymy of "uninterested" and "disinterested"? "Uninterested" used to mean "bored," and "disinterested" used to mean "impartial"—a valuable distinction that some people still make. I can understand, then, why people hate to see such useful tools of the language disappear. But that is certainly not the basis for Newman's distress over the increasing popularity of the idiom "convince to."

Apparently Newman feels that there was a golden age when language was Right, when it was in its ideal form. Probably that was the usage Newman learned so the golden age must have been sometime this century. But let's take a broader perspective; let's look beyond this century.

How did language start? Was it handed to us complete, a divinely designed thing, something that was as neatly logical as a system of mathematics? Of course not. It *evolved*. Perhaps cave men were dancing before a fire and uttered some singing sounds; perhaps they used noises to help with group hunting. We can only speculate. But surely language had humble beginnings. Words and phrases evolved. Grammar evolved. Even thinking evolved—probably the words helped us think better.[6]

Let me illustrate language's evolution. Here, believe it or not, is some English from about eight hundred years ago. Can you understand it?

> Fader ure, þu þe ert on heofene, Sye þin name gehalged. Tobecume þin rice. Gewurðe þin gewille on eorðan, swa swa on heofenan.[7]

Did you recognize the Lord's Prayer: "Our Father, who art in heaven...." Newman's concern with "convince to"—and the implication of a static, ideal language—seems a little silly, doesn't it?

Even Shakespeare, who wrote about four hundred years ago, wrote an older version of our language, one that is sometimes hard for us to understand today until we become acquainted with it. For example, do you know that "wherefore" means "why"? When Juliet says "O Romeo, Romeo! Wherefore art thou Romeo?" she isn't looking for him behind a tree. She's upset that he has to be, of all people, Romeo Montague, a member of the family that her family is feuding with: "Why must you be Romeo?"

There are other indications that our language isn't moving away from some divinely inspired ideal. Do you know that we didn't have a good English dictionary until 1755 when Samuel Johnson published one (he wrote it all himself)? Or that the prototypical English grammar dates from only 1762 with Bishop Lowth's *A Short Introduction to English Grammar?* So again, the question arises: Just what is Newman's source for his pronouncements on English usage?

The people who study language, linguists, know that Newman and his kind are ridiculous. In a foreword to Jim Quinn's book on the subject, *American Tongue and Cheek*, Benjamin DeMott says this: "Quinn shows the absolutists up for what they are:

pompous opportunists with a weak grasp of the nature of language, and a pathetic longing to be perceived as the last true gentlemen of Western Culture."[8] Quinn calls Newman, and others like him, a "pop grammarian."[9] And he specifically refers to Newman as "our leading, but not only, Chicken Little."[10] You know, "Language is falling! Language is falling!"

Another writer, John Trimble, characterizes such grammarians as literary prudes:

> Upon arrival at their mental state, they were at once ushered into a large congregation of true-believers whose faith is embalmed Formal English. Unaccountably, until now their faith has gone nameless. I will repair that oversight and christen it "The One True English Language Sect" (or "TOTELS" for short).[11]

Trimble then gives them a creed:

> We believe in Rules, Authority, and the One True English Language.
>
> We believe in the sanctity of Formal English, which shall ever be revered for its elaborate syntax, baroque sentences, ornate words, and stiff expressions, all of which we pledge ourselves laboriously to employ.
>
> Above all, we believe that naturalness is unnatural, that informality is unacceptable, and that individuality is unpardonable. Amen.[12]

And Joseph Williams, a contemporary writer who no doubt feels strong sympathy with Quinn and Trimble, makes a strong attack on the "pop grammar" he finds in William Zinsser's book, *On Writing Well.* Here's what Williams says in an article called "The Phenomenology of Error":

> I am often puzzled by what we call errors of grammar and usage, errors such as "different than," "between you and I," a "which" for a "that," and so on. I am puzzled by what motive could underlie the unusual ferocity which an "irregardless" or a "hopefully" or a singular "media" can elicit. In his second edition of *On Writing Well* (New York, 1980), William Zinsser, an otherwise amiable man, I'm sure, uses, and quotes not disapprovingly, words like "detestable vulgarity" (p. 43), "garbage"

(p. 44), "atrocity" (p. 46), "horrible" (p. 48), "oaf" (p. 42), "idiot" (p. 43), and "simple illiteracy" (p. 46), to comment on usages like "OK," "hopefully," the affix "-wise" and "myself" in "He invited Mary and myself to dinner."

The last thing I want to seem is sanctimonious. But I am sure Zinsser would agree, what happens in Cambodia and Afghanistan could more reasonably be called horrible atrocities. The likes of Idi Amin qualify as legitimate oafs. Idiots we have more than enough of in our state institutions. And while simple illiteracy is the condition of billions, it does not characterize those who use "disinterested" in its original sense.[13]

So don't let the pop grammarians intimidate you. They are full of little prescriptions for your writing, but those prescriptions come mainly from the pop grammarians themselves. Worse, the prescriptions are more likely to kill than to cure. For if you worry about the myriad of usage rules (which even the pop grammarians can't agree on), if you worry about being ridiculed by a local Edwin Newman, if you distort your writing to accommodate something other than expressing yourself clearly and well, then you have added a tyrant to your writing process. And this tyrant will cause in you the same kind of mental blockage I had when I tried to write "textbookese."

Misconception: Your Readers Know All of the "Rules"

I've just spent considerable time debunking the pop grammarians. But I don't want you to believe that there are absolutely no rules for using the English language. Of course there are rules. But you probably know most of the important ones: start sentences with capital letters and end them with periods, question marks, or exclamation points; spell words correctly; make sure subjects and verbs agree; and so forth. Then there are some slightly less important rules that most educated people follow, but that some don't, such as saying "for you and me" but not "for you and I" or such as using "whom" in the right place (although most professional writers try to avoid "whom" so they don't sound stuffy). However, there are only a few of these rules. Then there are the so-called rules of the pop grammarians—multitudes of these rules—which no one person could ever follow.

Joseph Williams, who wrote a good textbook on business writing called *Style: Ten Lessons in Clarity and Grace,* tells an interesting story about his book. While the book was still unpublished, he and a publisher sent it to college professors for their comments. Williams tells us of the results:

> With one exception, the reviewers, all teachers at universities, agreed that an intelligent treatment of error would be useful, and that this manuscript was at least in the ballpark. But almost every reader took exception to one item of usage that they thought I had been too soft on, that I should have unequivocally condemned as a violation of good usage. Unfortunately, each of them mentioned a different item.[14]

The implication? It is not that people are out there looking for as many errors as they can find, so we should therefore be careful to follow every bit of advice by Edwin Newman and John Simon. Rather, the implication is that even the "authorities" can't agree on what's important and what isn't. Some like this and some like that. As a result, we are free to ignore the pop grammarian's pets and to concentrate on expressing ourselves clearly and accurately.

This is not mere idealism, either. You may work for someone who seems to be a pop grammarian in his own right. From my experience, these people usually have only a few special concerns. I remember working for someone who didn't like the words "very" and "quite." He felt he needed no emphasis to his pronouncements—his merest wish was everyone else's command. To use "very" and "quite" made him, in his mind, seem weak, pleading. Well . . . we humored him, of course. But we would have been mistaken to have gone further, to have assumed that this was a man who had in his mind all of the writing "pets" we had ever come across. We would have been mistaken to have tried to be extra-correct in everything that we wrote for his signature. If English teachers can't agree, if pop grammarians can't agree, then our bosses and our readers can't, either. And since there is no generally accepted set of these rules available, then we should concentrate on something else. As you will see in the next chapter, freeing yourself from such invidious concerns will help remove the blockage in the writing process.

Misconception: Some Writing Must Be Difficult to Be Precise

This is a common excuse people give to justify their bad writing. Lawyers are probably the most likely of all to give such an excuse. David Mellinkoff, in *The Language of the Law*, spends about a hundred pages refuting this point. He writes, "Lawyers have been telling each other for so many years that the language of the law is *precise* that they have come to believe it"—even though they have been taking each other to court continuously for the language they have been using.[15]

Mellinkoff then comments, usually humorously, on many of the words and phrases that the lawyers hold so dear. For example, consider "aforesaid." Just what does it mean—the previous word, the one before that, the previous section, what? Mellinkoff then cites court cases in which lawyers have fought over that very word.[16] So much for its preciseness.

When we are expressing ourselves in language that might be scrutinized by lawyers, we must, of course, be careful, we must be precise. Occasionally, a writer in such circumstances might have to use some technical words—some words in the law and elsewhere certainly can carry precise definitions. Fine. Use them when you should. But those few words need not cause the whole of the writing to be unreadable.

Misconception: Some Ideas Are Too Complicated to Express Clearly

I think that Ludwig Wittgenstein has the perfect answer to this one:

> Everything that can be thought at all can be thought clearly.
> Everything that can be said can be said clearly.[17]

That's pretty hard to refute, isn't it?

Wittgenstein doesn't mean that we should therefore be able to communicate everything to everybody. If, for example, a mathematician tries to explain to me his latest breakthrough in theoretical calculus, he'd have real trouble. First, he would have to give me a rather thorough refresher course in calculus so I could even begin to understand him. But if he were talking to a colleague in calculus, he should be able to express himself clearly.

Most of the time, bad government, military, business, and academic writing is unclear even to the "colleague"—often people like you and me, people the writer expects to communicate with.

The excuse, then, that someone's writing has to be unclear because the ideas are "profound" doesn't make much sense. Nor does the related idea that the writer must simply be on a higher intellectual plane than we are, or else we'd understand him. Just refer him to Wittgenstein's quotation.

MOVING BEYOND THE
MISCONCEPTIONS

This chapter has been aimed at helping you gain a new perspective on writing and language. Too many people feel so intimidated by language, consciously or unconsciously afraid of being ridiculed by "Edwin Newman," that they try harder to be correct than to be clear and accurate. And those who have trouble writing clearly sometimes hide behind their "profundity" or their need for "preciseness." But, as we have seen, there is rarely a good reason for producing writing that is hard for your reader to read.

Now let's end with a "test." Here's a newspaper article that's a perfect example of "pop grammar"—the kind that should provoke, though it's not intended to, laughter instead of "grave concern." See how many logical inconsistencies you can find:

From "Bob Levey's Washington"

In this corner, we never drop our guard, even on national holidays [this article appeared on Labor Day, 1982]. So I lace up my gloves and prepare to take on Patricia Myers, columnist for *Publisher's Auxiliary*, a newspaper published here by the National Newspaper Association.

Patricia rises in defense of the misuse of "hopefully." It is hoped that I can make her see the light.

Patricia doesn't argue that wrong is right. In the sentence, "Hopefully, the rain will end soon," there is a clear wrong [many linguists would disagree], and Patricia admits it. The word "hopefully" modifies rain, when the speaker really wants it to describe the mood of the person gazing at the sky. Rendered more carefully [in this very sentence, the writer makes a similar mistake to the one he has just decried—unless, of

course, he really means that Patricia has been "rendered"],
Patricia points out that the sentence should read, "I hope that
the rain will end soon."

However, several cousins of "hopefully" are misused every
day, and few people so much as twitch, says Patricia. Take, for
example, the phrase, "Luckily, the bear was killed before he at-
tacked the little boy." As Patricia notes, you hardly mean that
the bear was lucky.

But to Patricia, the more compelling argument is this: the
popularity of "misused hopefully" has earned it a place in lit-
erate circles.

"We don't have another word that means the same thing,"
she writes. "Almost everyone uses it, it's understandable in its
context and it's no more intrinsically illogical" than misuses of
"fortunately," "happily" and "luckily." Therefore, open your
arms and embrace it, citizenry.

Not this kid.

I don't believe a grammar book is a bible, setting forth im-
mutable rules for all time. Words are born and die. Idioms wax
and wane. Rules are forever being adjusted according to popular demand.

But to condone the misuse of "hopefully" is to condone im-
precision [!!!]. In "Hopefully, the rain will end soon," I'm pretty
sure I know what the speaker or writer is trying to say. But I'm
not as sure as I would be if the sentence was: "I hope that the
rain will end soon."

Isn't the whole idea to communicate as clearly as we can? If
a writer or speaker leaves unnecessary ambiguities, he'll soon
find there's no one reading or listening.

Patricia is right in one respect. We don't have another word
that means the same thing as the "incorrect" usage of "hopefully." But do we have to restrict the hunt for clarity to individual words? We have any number of phrases that would get
across our wish that it would stop raining. Are we in such a
hurry that only single words will do?

Finally, I'm unimpressed with the comparison of "hopefully" to the misuses of "fortunately," "happily" and "luckily."
Reminds me of Richard Nixon's staff during Watergate. Remember how they defended the behavior of the White House
"plumbers" by arguing that every administration bent or broke
the rules? That didn't make it right, and it doesn't make the
misuse of "hopefully" right.[18]

Imagine the fun that Jim Quinn, John Trimble, and Joseph Williams could have with "pop grammar" such as this.

Notes for Chapter 2

1. Maxine Hairston, *A Contemporary Rhetoric*, 2nd ed. (Boston: Houghton Mifflin, 1978), p. 3.

2. Hairston, p. 4.

3. Thomas S. Kuhn, *The Structure of Scientific Revolutions*, 2nd ed., enlarged (Chicago: University of Chicago Press, 1970), p. 1.

4. Edwin Newman, *Strictly Speaking: Will America Be the Death of English?* (New York: Warner Books, 1974), p. 47.

5. For an interesting discussion of the impact of *Webster's Third New International Dictionary*, which caused a furor because of its alleged shift from being a lawgiver to being a historian, I recommend James Sledd's "The Lexicographer's Uneasy Chair," *College English*, 23, No. 8 (May 1962), 682-87. Sledd defends the dictionary.

6. Lev Vygotsky, in *Thought and Language*, trans. and ed. Eugenia Hanfmann and Gertrude Vakar (Cambridge, Massachusetts: The M. I. T. Press, 1962), examines with considerable profundity the interrelation of thought and language. Vygotsky believes that thought and language have entirely separate beginnings. Children develop an egocentric speech, which by the time they are six or seven gradually moves into the mind as nonverbal inner speech—thinking in words.

I'd also like to add here a comment that even though language probably began in rather simple circumstances—like the hunt or songs around a campfire—I don't mean to imply that language began simply and then became increasingly complex. It may have begun simply, but our language today is considerably simpler than Old English, which had far fewer regular forms of words. To use the terminology, it was "highly inflected."

7. *History of the English Language*, ed. Richard L. Hoffman (Boston: Little, Brown, 1968), p. 33.

8. Benjamin DeMott, Foreword, *American Tongue and Cheek*, by Jim Quinn (New York: Penguin Books, 1980), p. x. DeMott does not agree with some of Quinn's points in the book, but he clearly agrees with Quinn on his attitude toward the pop grammarians.

9. Jim Quinn, *American Tongue and Cheek* (New York: Penguin Books, 1980), p. xvi. Quinn, who has separate chapters on Newman and Simon, is a strong antidote for those who believe in pop grammar. He relies on the *Oxford English Dictionary* (*OED*) to refute people like Newman. It is important to note that Quinn doesn't treat the *OED* as a bigger and better authority on what is right; rather, he shows that over the years there have been so many different meanings, or usages, of any word that people like Newman are ridiculous to insist on any single meaning or usage as *the* correct one.

10. Quinn, p. 20.

11. John R. Trimble, *Writing with Style: Conversations on the Art of Writing* (Englewood Cliffs, New Jersey: Prentice-Hall, 1975), p. 84. The entire Chapter 9, "Superstitions," is superb.

12. Trimble, p. 85.

13. Joseph M. Williams, "The Phenomenology of Error," *College Composition and Communication,* 32 (May 1981), 152.

14. Williams, 155.

15. David Mellinkoff, *The Language of the Law* (Boston: Little, Brown and Company, 1963), p. 290.

16. Mellinkoff, pp. 305-306.

17. Ludwig Wittgenstein, quoted by Joseph Williams in *Style: Ten Lessons in Clarity and Grace* (Glenview, Illinois: Scott, Foresman and Co., 1981), p. 1.

18. Bob Levey, "Bob Levey's Washington," *The Washington Post,* September 6, 1982, p. D17.

3 HOW WE WRITE

Writing is a highly individual process. We all have our own ways, and even the best writers would hardly agree on a single "right" way. On the other hand, the best writers could probably discover many areas of agreement.

Let me make an analogy. Golfers have standards for how to swing a driver or a seven iron, but they seem to feel that putting is up to the individual. While putting, a golfer can develop his own stroke, and whatever is most comfortable, whatever seems to work for him, is all right. Writing is a skill like putting in that whatever seems to work for any one person is all right.

Yet most golfers, while putting, do many things alike: they flex their knees slightly, they hold their putter with both hands fairly high on the shaft, they take the putter straight back, and they follow through toward the hole. But then there's an occasional Sam Snead who has decided he'll do things his own way, facing the hole instead of standing sideways to it, and holding the putter with one hand far down the shaft.

In writing, too, most people who are successful do many things alike, although there are a few "Sam Sneads" who seem to succeed by their own eccentric methods. Perhaps they succeed because of those methods, or perhaps in spite of them.

For this chapter, I'll present a commonly accepted model of the writing process, one that most of the good writers I know tend to follow. Then I will tell you of some contemporary ideas in the writing field which do not contradict the model in any way but which can make it work *significantly* better for you. In fact, the model without these contemporary additions is only a half-truth. But we'll start with the half-truth and then add the other half to it.

A MODEL FOR WRITING

Think of writing as a process divided into three stages: prewriting, writing, and rewriting.

In the *prewriting* stage, you gather all of your information together, perhaps by reading and taking notes, by making phone calls, by looking through the files, by talking to other people, or even just by collecting your thoughts. Afterward, you may wish to make some sort of an outline. This may be no more than an informal list of the key points you want to be sure to mention or something more formal and considerably more complete. As you'll see later in this chapter, though, you're likely to make a mistake if you try to perfect your organization at this stage of the process.

In the *writing* stage, you make a quick first draft of whatever you're writing. Concentrate on the big things, like the overall organization, the movement from idea to idea, the relationship of the parts to the whole. Don't worry about such details as punctuation or getting the exact word. If you do, you'll distract yourself from those larger matters.

In the *rewriting* stage, you can worry about both the smaller and the larger matters. You can spend time getting the exact word and deciding whether or not you need a comma—such details now won't distract you from the paper's overall flow since you already established that during the writing stage. You can also worry about the larger matters. Most good writers like to set their work aside for awhile—hours perhaps, but sometimes days if practical (which it often isn't). By setting your draft aside, you allow yourself to take a fresh look at it later, almost as if someone else had written it. You can then spot some amazing things that you hadn't even noticed before. This stage, rewriting, is a good time to fiddle with the writing. It's probably the least demanding, mentally, of all three stages, but it is also very important.

You may wish to go through the writing and rewriting stages several times if what you're writing is long. If you're writing a twenty-page report, for example, you'd probably wish to do the prewriting for the entire report before you started. But you might wish to write a section of the report and revise that at least once before going on to the next section.

A RECURSIVE PROCESS

So far, I've presented writing as though it's a *linear* process: first the prewriting, then the writing, then the rewriting. I think that's *one* convenient way to think of the writing process, but it would often be a mistake for us to try to write that way. Like most human activities, writing is more complex than it seems.

Think of writing also as a *recursive* process: that is, instead of prewriting, writing, and rewriting taking place one after another, think of them constantly looping back on one another.

For example, prewriting—planning what we wish to say— occurs not only at the very beginning of the writing process but throughout. Think about when you write. Don't you often have long pauses when you're planning the shape of the rest of your paper?

The same is true for revision. You almost certainly don't do all of your revision at the end, even though you may do a substantial portion then. You're revising constantly as you go along.

Nancy Sommers, who has done considerable research on the writing process, talks about revision this way:

> Current research offers a contradictory perspective to the conventional conception that revision is a separate activity that comes after the completion of the first draft and one that can be singularly distinguished from the conception, incubation, or production components of the process. One constantly revises as one writes, as one tries to make a work congruent with what one intends. This is a process that occurs

prior to and throughout the writing of a work as a writer continues to be surprised and enlightened by his own words and ideas.[1]

Think of the writing process in two ways, then: Think of it taking place, roughly, in the large blocks of prewriting, writing, and rewriting, which is a *linear* model. But also think of those three components constantly intermixing and returning on one another.

WRITING AS THINKING

If you've done much writing, you've probably had the experience of discovering to your chagrin that what seemed clear when you were thinking it just didn't seem clear at all when you tried to put it on paper. That's a common experience, and it probably happens to almost everybody all the time, to one extent or another, except during the most routine writing.

Today's writing specialists see writing as a thinking process. In other words, when you are at the point of actually putting words on paper, when your brain is actively engaged with the details of your material during the writing stage, you are not simply transcribing your thoughts. You are also shaping and reshaping them, rethinking, revising, analyzing. To some extent, in fact, you don't really know what you think until you try to write it.

In an excellent book on writing, something of a minor classic in the field, Peter Elbow presents a nice image for this phenomenon:

> Meaning is not what you start out with but what you end up with. Control, coherence, and knowing your mind are not what you start out with but what you end up with. Think of writing then not as a way to transmit a message but as a way to grow and cook a message.[2]

Elbow has another good image for the writing process: "Producing writing ... is not so much like filling a basin or a pool once, but rather getting water to flow *through* till it finally runs clear."[3]

If much of the important part of thinking—the "growing" and "cooking" of your message—occurs when you're writing that first draft, what is the implication for the writing process? The important implication is that you should not overdo the prewriting stage. If you try to force yourself to write a complete, detailed, and perfect outline, you may well be doing so before your thoughts have clarified. Then if you're the persevering type and stick with that outline no matter what, you will probably force a lot of square pegs into round holes.

Should you make an outline at all in the prewriting stage? I do. And, actually, I sometimes get fairly complete, particularly if I'm writing something lengthy. On the other hand, I don't *worry* myself over the outline. Sometimes, in fact, I don't consult it at all when I'm doing the actual writing. The value of the outline, for me, comes before and after the writing stage. Before the writing stage, it helps me gather all of the material into my head at once, saturating myself with it. It also gives me a sense of where to start, where to end, and how to cover the points in between.

While I'm doing the actual writing, I let the ideas come as they will. Often a natural organization develops, rather than an "imposed" one if I had stuck with the outline: during the writing stage, I am "inside" the material, grappling with it first-hand; during the pre-writing stage, I am still mainly "outside" it.

An advantage of the natural organization that develops during the writing stage is that the ideas seem to move better from one to the other—I'm following one thread all the way through, each idea following naturally from the one before it.

I also said that I use the outline after the writing stage. Once I finish my first draft, I glance through my outline to see that I haven't left out anything important. I'm often surprised at how many of my major points became small ones, and how many small points grew.

THE ROLE OF THE UNCONSCIOUS

Many people probably think of inspiration as a message from the gods, but it is more likely a message from their own unconscious.

The traditional—outdated—view of the writing process seemed to take into account only the conscious part of the brain: brain activity took place only during writing activity, and writing activity took place only when the seat of the pants was applied to the seat of the chair. Today, however, we understand that the unconscious part of the mind plays a much larger role than most of us suspected.

Have you ever had a thought strike you "from out of the blue," one that provided you with a new direction or solved a problem for you? This phenomenon isn't restricted to writing, of course. It can happen when you're making a career choice, worrying over a personal problem, trying to figure out how to repair that lawnmower that frustrated you yesterday.

Or it can happen with writing. William Irmscher has a good description of this phenomenon in his book, *Teaching Expository Writing:*

> Mulling over a project can be productive, not because it leads anywhere immediately, but because it sets into motion a subconscious or pre-conscious activity that has a way of operating without our awareness of it. The result is often an idea or hunch or grasp that comes as an illumination—nothing necessarily revelatory, but an insight that comes with such suddenness that we are tempted to think of it as a reward for our obsessiveness.[4]

The idea that the unconscious can provide us with important insight is not a new one, of course, though only in the past decade or so has it gained both acceptance and application in the field of writing. Here's an excerpt from a book written over fifty years ago by Graham Wallas which has influenced writing specialists today. In it, Wallas tells a story of the German physicist, Helmholtz:

> Helmholtz . . . speaking in 1891 at a banquet on his seventieth birthday, described the way in which his most important new thoughts had come to him. He said that after previous investigation of the problem "in all directions . . . happy ideas came unexpectedly without effort, like an inspiration. So far as I am concerned, they have never come to me while my mind was fatigued, or when I was at my working table. . . . They came particularly readily during the slow ascent of wooded hills on a sunny day." Helmholtz here gives us three stages in the formation of a new thought. The first in time I shall call Preparation, the stage during which the problem was "investigated . . . in all directions"; the second is the stage during which he was not consciously thinking about the problem, which I shall call

Incubation; the third, consisting of the appearance of the
"happy idea" together with the psychological events which
immediately preceded and accompanied that appearance, I
shall call Illumination.

And I shall add a fourth stage, of Verification, which Helmholtz does not here mention . . . in which both the validity of
the idea was tested, and the idea itself was reduced to exact
form.[5]

Wallas divides the creative process, then, into these four
stages: Preparation, Incubation, Illumination (or Inspiration), and
Verification.

Again, you may wonder if this has any application to the writing process. After all, inspiration doesn't seem like something that
we can control. In a way, that's true. Our minds are not like computers, something we can turn on instantly, operate for hours at a
consistently high efficiency, or even turn off at will. As William
Irmscher says of inspiration, "We are grateful when it occurs, but
we do not rely on it."[6]

Yet we can almost rely on it. Experiment with yourself sometime. When you run into a problem in any stage of the writing
process—getting a preliminary outline together, starting the next
section in your first draft, figuring out how to make a point more
clearly while you are editing—stop. Be sure that you have "satura-
ted" yourself with the pertinent information; that is, review the
problem in your mind so that your mind is filled with the necessary details, and then stop. You will then be at the "preparation"
stage, what Helmholtz referred to as investigating the problem "in
all directions."

Next, do something that is less intellectually demanding,
something relaxing; if it's night, quit and don't start again until
morning. You will then be ready for your mind to start the "incubation" phase, the time Helmholtz walked slowly up the wooded hill
on a sunny day.

The "illumination" can occur at any time—or, infrequently,
not at all. I recommend that if it occurs, jot your ideas down. Illu-
minations seem to be quite perishable.

Finally, check to be sure your illumination actually works. See
if it really solves your problem. This is the fourth stage, "verification."

I recommend, then, that you consciously use your unconscious—that you consciously use the creative process to aid your writing. The creative process can be helpful, as I said, at any of the three stages of the writing process. I think it can be particularly helpful during the actual writing, though, when your mind is most actively struggling with the details of your material. That is the time a roadblock is most likely to occur. If at all possible, simply stop and allow your unconscious to do its work. That's what most good writers do.

FINDING YOUR VOICE

The single biggest breakthrough you can make in improving your writing is finding your writing personality, sometimes called "finding your voice." If you can make that breakthrough, you will discover that the words can come easily and quickly. It seems almost as though you are talking on paper. The ideas seem to come directly from your mind to the page, without passing through any filter, or any editing stage. It is as though your ideas had passed through a constricted pipe—one partially blocked—and then the blockage was removed and the ideas flowed freely.

In Chapter 1, I told you the story of my first book. When I tried to write in an artificial textbook style, I was unable to get any words on paper; but when I imagined myself sitting on the edge of my desk and talking to my class, suddenly the words came easily. I had "found my voice" for the first time.

I like to think of this voice as one aspect of my personality, the expression of who I am when I am writing. When I was writing that first book, I tried to be something I was not: a writer of textbookese. Then when I let myself be something I was—a teacher talking to his class—I was able to use my own voice, to express my own personality.

But what is the relationship between a voice and a personality? I think that we have established numerous roles, or personalities, for ourselves that we use every day. We have one role that fits us when we are with our close friends, another for children, others for parents, teachers, car salesmen, medical doctors, large or small groups we are speaking to. We are at our best when we are comfortable in the roles we are filling. If we've bought several cars, we know how we wish to behave when we bargain for a new one; if we've spoken before large groups frequently, we know how to behave then. We know what role fits us.

Now I have been using the term "role" as though it is a mask we put on to fool others into thinking we are something we are not. That's not what I mean at all. All of these "roles" can be sincerely us, if we're reasonably well adjusted. Think of a role as "a subset of the total self"—we can't be everything at once.[7] One criterion of maturity, in fact, is how well we can choose the appropriate behavior, or role, for a given set of circumstances.

Some of these roles take quite a while to develop. First, our overall personality hardly settles down until sometime after we have gone through the trauma of adolescence, though certainly plenty of the raw material for that personality was there all along. But specific roles—like the role of a writer—also need time and the right circumstances to develop.

You may wonder why people have trouble developing a personality that will make their writing easier. Think back on the writing you have done. You no doubt began in school and, sad to say, many school experiences do not help a person develop a writing personality. Here's an excerpt from a research project conducted in England in the 1970s. This report and its predecessor have influenced many teachers in this country.

> The trouble with most school writing is that it is not genuine communication. When adults write they are usually trying to tell someone something he doesn't already know; when children write in school they are usually writing for someone who, they are well aware, knows better than they do what they are trying to say and who is concerned to evaluate their attempt to say it. Even when they are writing a story, when the teacher does not know better than they do what they are saying, the response of the teacher is so often to the surface features of spelling, punctuation and handwriting. So once again the teacher is seen as an assessor and not as someone interested in being communicated with.[8]

Too many people who have finished school are still trying to please their teachers—are still more worried about being "correct" than about expressing themselves clearly. As a result, they create a block in the writing process, a block in that pipe that leads from the brain to the paper.

I like to think of this block as an "interposed editor": between the brain and the paper, some people have a tenth grade school teacher who monitors every word to be sure it is correct enough and impressive enough. When I was first writing that first book, I had an interposed editor who was trying to convert my ideas to textbook writing.

Yet this "editor" is entirely unnecessary. Worse, it slows the writing and when the writing does struggle through, that editor converts it into something unnatural and unreadable.

How do we get rid of this editor? First, we have to realize that the editor isn't really improving anything. The purpose of the previous chapter on misconceptions about writing was to make you feel that you can express yourself more naturally, more informally, without being ridiculed by a local Edwin Newman or a tenth grade teacher. Second, you must ask yourself as you write, "How would I *say* this to someone if he were right here in front of me?" Then write it that way. Take out the "ums" and the "you knows," of course, and take advantage of the extra time you have when writing instead of speaking to get your ideas just right. I'll have more on exactly how to do this in Chapter 5.

CONSIDERING YOUR AUDIENCE

If you're fortunate enough to find the right voice, the right personality, you also need a good understanding of the needs of your reader. If you've read much about writing, you're no doubt familiar with the dictum that you must always be aware of your audience. That is good advice, but I'm afraid that not many people understand it.

As we mature, we become less and less egocentric. As babies, we're aware almost solely of our own needs, and we'll do whatever it takes to get them met—screaming in public being a quite popular method. As young children, we believe that others think exactly as we do so that if we talk about Freddy, meaning our teddy bear, we think that everybody should know just what we mean.

Some people never quite outgrow that essential egocentricity. I am reminded of an acquaintance from Buffalo, New York, who was astounded to find out that I had never been to Niagara Falls. He lived so close to it that he thought it must be part of every person's experience. Some writers are provincial in the same way.

A mark of an intelligent writer, then, is understanding just what his readers do and do not know. In fact, I think good writers are aware of both a specific audience and a more general one.

Good writers, of course, consider the knowledge and the other specific characteristics of the specific audience they're writing to. Just how much do your readers know about your subject, and just how much do they need to know? Will they look upon it favorably from the beginning, or will they need a little extra persuading?

But perhaps more important, good writers are aware of the needs of audiences in general. As we will see in Chapters 8 and 9, all readers need examples, transitions, and a certain amount of redundancy if they are to understand your writing. With experience as a writer, with maturity in dealing with other people, and with the understanding that other people aren't mind readers, you can develop what is called a "generalized other"—a model within your mind for readers in general.[9]

In a way, you have to create this "generalized other" the same way you create the role for yourself as a writer: as a writer, you adopt a certain aspect of your own personality that allows you to write easily; but to communicate well, you must also create a personality to write to. In a way, this other personality is your listener, your reader, your general and omni-present audience. Only a mature person can create this fantasy audience, with its capabilities and limitations; and only a mature *writer* has actually succeeded in creating it.

One of your primary goals as a writer should be to create and internalize this audience, this "generalized other," to make your writing unconsciously and automatically aimed toward it. That is not an easy thing to do, but the specific writing skills I recommend in the second part of this book will start you on your way.

I ended the last chapter with a "test," showing you an example of "pop grammar" in action. I'd like to end this chapter by showing you the damage that teachers, perhaps with good intentions, can do to young students. Here's an essay by a young British student. It's terribly marred with mechanical errors, yet the content of the essay is moving, showing control and care—despite the teacher's comment, which I will give you later. So read this essay, trying to ignore the errors. In fact, to appreciate the essay's power, I suggest you read it aloud or have someone read it aloud to you.:

The Hunt

A small fox was playing in the wood's with various odd's & end's that he found lying around when, he heard a sound that sent a chill's down his spine, it was the sound of dog's barking & he knew they were after him. So he started to run. but he had nowhere much to run to & not much time so he ran toward's the thick part of the wood that is more like a jungle than a wood. He ran as fast as his leg's would carry him, though the hounds were gaining on him but, he made it to the thick part of the wood which would help him, & slow the huntsmen & dog's down. He ran through bushe's, bramble's, pile's of leave's & hedge's, he leaped fellen tree's & pieces of rubbish left by stupid untidy picknicker's that had visited the wood's. He ran along tree trunks, & the narrowist of path's between tree's, through barbed wire and under gates but still he could hear that awful yapping of the hound's & the sound of horn's and shout's of huntsmen urging the dogs and horses to go faster. By now the little fox was beginning to get tired so he ran towards an old house where he knew there was a hole in the wall for him to hide in. He reached it and rushed into the house & hid in his hole. There he waited shaking & nearly frightened to death. He knew they would find him and kill him.

The hound's were getting closer & closer & he knew death was near,but then a funny thing happened, the sound of the hound's was getting further away. they weren't chasing him any more, or maybe they were chasing something else & not him. Anyway to him it didn't matter, it wasn't his turn to die.[10]

Now for the teacher's comments: "I'm not very impressed. Your work is *mediocre*, lacking real control and care. You will force me to take the matter up with other staff unless you produce work of a higher quality."

The point is not that matters of spelling and so forth aren't important. They are, of course. Surely these matters interfered with your reading of the story. The point is that these matters are not the *only* things important. The teacher in this instance has totally ignored the communication.

By the way, you can surely understand why the boy would write such a story, can't you? If he is the fleeing fox, who do you suppose is the hound?

Notes for Chapter 3

1. Nancy Sommers, "Response to Sharon Crowley, 'Components of the Composing Process,'" *CCC*, 29 (May 1978), 209.

In another article—"Revision Strategies of Student Writers and Experienced Adult Writers," *CCC*, 31 (Dec 1980), 378-87—Sommers notes that student and experienced writers have entirely different concepts of revision. The adults often think about "reseeing" their essay; the students, on the other hand, are more likely to think about simple word changes:

> The students have strategies for handling words and phrases and their strategies helped them on a word and sentence level. What they lack, however, is a set of strategies to help them identify the "something larger" that they sensed was wrong and work from there. The students do not have strategies for handling the whole essay. (p. 383)

Linda Flower and John Hayes have also done some excellent, provocative work in analyzing the writing process. I especially recommend their article "A Cognitive Process Theory of Writing," *CCC*, 32 (Dec 1981), 365-387.

2. Peter Elbow, *Writing without Teachers* (London: Oxford University Press, 1973), p. 15. Elbow is a proponent of free writing—that is, writing, writing, and writing without stopping, opening the pipeline from the brain to the paper, getting thoughts on paper and making sense of them later.

3. Elbow, p. 28.

4. William F. Irmscher, *Teaching Expository Writing* (New York: Holt, Rinehart and Winston, 1979), p. 31. Irmscher calls the unconscious "intuition." He believes that intuition "derives from both living experiences and experiences with languages" (p. 34). Therefore, it is something that we can improve. The more we know about our subject, or the more we know about writing, the higher the quality of our intuitive insights.

5. Graham Wallas, *The Art of Thought* (New York: Harcourt Brace Jovanovich, 1926), pp. 79-81. Quoted in Janet Emig's *The Composing Process of Twelfth*

Graders, NCTE Research Report No. 13 (Urbana, Illinois: National Council of Teachers of English, 1971), p. 17.

6.   Irmscher, p. 32.

7.   I am indebted to Professor Richard Lloyd-Jones for this insight.

8.   Nancy Martin, et al., *Writing and Learning across the Curriculum 11-16,* Schools Council Writing across the Curriculum Project, University of London Institute of Education (London: Hollen Street Press, 1976), p. 29.

9.   James Britton, et al., *The Development of Writing Abilities (11-18)* (London: MacMillen, 1975), p. 62. As Professor Richard Lloyd-Jones points out, there's more involved than simply having a writer and a "generalized other." The writer must also have a good *relationship* with this generalized other. For example, to write easily, informally, the writer must not only understand his audience, but he also must feel some confidence in facing it. Once again, that takes us back to the psychological maturity we have been discussing in this chapter.

10.   Martin, pp. 104-5.

4   HOW WE READ

Now let's turn from how we write to how we read. You may wonder why you should concern yourself with reading since you learned how to read in the first grade, and your interest now, and presumably mine, is writing and not reading. Fair questions, but the answers are easy. In fact, this may be the most important chapter you will read in this book.

I believe that clear writing is writing that is easy for the reader to—in the psycholinguistic jargon—"process." In other words, clear writing is writing that is easy for the reader to read. A few decades ago that statement might have been nice enough, and true enough, but we could only have nodded our heads gravely and then turned back to writing and forgotten about the reading. However, in the past ten or fifteen years, as linguists and psychologists have become interested, there have been tremendous advances in the study of how we read. So if you think of reading theory as the province of commercial establishments out to make a quick buck or of Miss Fidditch who taught you in elementary school, then you're in for a surprise. In fact, as I began my research for this book, I was surprised, and the more I read about reading theory, the more fascinated I became.

For this chapter I'll present a simple model of the reading process—enough for you to feel you have an overall view of it—but I won't bog you down with irrelevant details. Occasionally, though, I will summarize specific psychological experiments that I think are particularly interesting. Then—and here is the important point—I will use the information that you will learn in this chapter constantly in the second part of the book, the part that recommends specific writing skills for you to adopt.

This chapter lays the theoretical groundwork I will return to time and again. It will help show you why, for example, writing short sentences (despite what you may have read elsewhere) often doesn't do a thing to make your writing, or anybody else's, easy to read. And the information in this chapter will also help explain such things as why passive voice isn't all that bad, just what we mean by "big" words, and much more.

First, though, a caution. As I said, serious scientific interest in reading theory is comparatively recent; therefore, the field is a long way from gaining consensus about even something as fundamental as a general model for how the reading process takes place. There has, of course, been experiment after experiment. Unfortunately, many of them have refuted others of them. However, there is consensus in a number of important areas—key areas for our purposes in this book.

A MODEL

I can remember believing such outdated notions about reading as these:

1.   Good readers make only a couple of eye fixations per line, taking in many words each time.

2.   Reading is simply adding up the meanings of the words on a page.

I said in the introduction to this chapter that there are many controversies in the field of reading theory; however, there isn't any controversy about the above points. Nobody with any expertise believes them any longer. The model shown in Figure 1 will help you understand why:

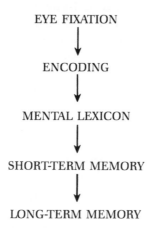

READING MATTER

EYE FIXATION

↓

ENCODING

↓

MENTAL LEXICON

↓

SHORT-TERM MEMORY

↓

LONG-TERM MEMORY

Figure 1.   A Model of the Reading Process

Reading Matter

By "reading matter" in the model, I mean simply books, magazines, newspapers, any material that someone can engage in reading.

Eye Fixation

Reading occurs through a series of eye fixations in which the eye sweeps in a series of jerks across the page. The eye cannot move smoothly, although it may appear to, but instead makes many stops. If you want to demonstrate this, make a pinhole in a piece of paper with writing on it. Then look through the hole at the eyes of someone else reading it. The jerky movements you see are called "saccades."

During these saccades, the reader cannot process any new reading material; the processing occurs solely at the stops. Also, at each new saccade the reader loses the image in his mind of the previous fixation—a fortunate occurrence, if you think about it, or else his mind would be very cluttered with images. This does not mean, however, that the reader has entirely lost contact with the information before the new saccade, only that the information has moved to a deeper level of processing.

Now, how many words can you see with each fixation (this will explain the first of the outdated notions above)? Actually, there is a physiological limit: about ten letters or spaces on either side of a fixation point. Try this test for yourself.[1] Not now, but as soon as you finish reading these brief directions, fix your eyes on the [X] in the center of the figure below. Then, without moving your eyes at all, see how much you can perceive to the right and left. Remember, don't let your eyes wander from the [X].

Go ahead:

ONE HOP SILK BUT EYE NOW   [X]   how far away can you see?

The letters get fuzzy to the right and left, don't they? However, you might be able to perceive the letters better to the right for two reasons: first, they are part of a meaningful sentence, so you can have some additional information to help you guess; second, since they are written in lower case letters, parts of which sometimes rise above or fall below the line, you have even more information for making your guess.

But what happens in practice? What happens to readers in actual reading situations? M. A. Just and P. A. Carpenter showed in an important experiment that readers trying to comprehend passages as well as possible (not trying, in other words, simply to skim) had an eye fixation an average of once every 1.2 content words.[2] (Content words are nouns, pronouns, verbs, adverbs, and adjectives—the words that seem to carry the most "meaning.") Figure 2 shows a passage from the experiment showing where the fixations took place for one typical college student. The durations of these fixations are recorded above the words in milliseconds. Above the milliseconds you can see the order of the fixations—in the second sentence, the reader moved his eyes back one time. As you can see, this reader had an eye fixation on almost every word in the passage.

1	2	3	4	5	6	7
1566	267	400	83	267	617	767
Flywheels	are	one	of the	oldest	mechanical	devices

8	9	1	2	3	5	4 6
450	450	400	616	517	684	250 317
known	to	man.	Every	internal-	combustion engine	contains

7	8	9	10	11		
617	1116	367	467	483		
a small	flywheel	that	converts	the	jerky motion	of the

12	13	14	15 16	17	18	19
450	383	284	383 317	283	533	50
pistons	into	the	smooth flow	of energy	that powers	the

20	21
366	566
drive	shaft.

Figure 2.   Sample Eye Fixations

Encoding

In the encoding step the brain converts what the eye perceives at a fixation on the page into a meaningful code that it can then use for further processing. There are a number of theories on exactly what happens here. Perhaps there is some step in which the reader mentally pronounces the word to himself? (Most researchers today agree that this does not happen; even relatively slow reading rates are much too fast to permit this.) Or perhaps the brain takes the word in whole, regardless of its parts? Or perhaps the brain breaks the word into its root, its prefix, and its suffix?[3]

Whatever the researchers finally decide, the important point for us to notice is that fluent readers rarely take in a word letter by letter, that they rarely read "h-o-r-s-e" instead of "horse" (except, of course, children at the very beginning stages of learning the alphabet and learning to read).[4] This point will become important later, in Chapter 8, when we talk about conciseness.

Mental Lexicon

Even though the brain *en*coded the fixation during the step I just discussed, it has not yet *de*coded the meaning. In other words, you still don't know what you're reading. So the next step in the reading process is for the brain to find out what the just encoded word or phrase means. The most prevalent theory today is that the brain keeps its own dictionary, called the "mental lexicon," where the brain looks up each word that it encodes.

Just how is this dictionary organized? Is it like *Webster's Third*, a huge, comprehensive thing containing all the words we know, however well or however slightly? Almost certainly not, according to the researchers. For one phenomenon that recurs time and again in experiments is that common words take significantly less time (speaking relatively here, for times are measured in milliseconds) for the reader to recognize than uncommon words.[5] Another frequently observed phenomenon is that readers spend less time recognizing an uncommon word if they've just run across it.

Apparently, our mental lexicon doesn't look much at all like a traditional dictionary; instead, the words are probably stored at various distances from a recognition threshold.[6] The common words are close to this threshold, the uncommon ones farther away. Then when the brain searches for the words—attempting, say, to decode a new fixation—the common words cross the threshold to recognition more quickly. This phenomenon will be quite important in Chapter 6 when we talk about using simpler words.

Short-Term Memory

The concepts of short-term memory and long-term memory have extremely important implications for readability.

First, let's start with the long-term memory. The long-term memory is, basically, what you might think of as everything you know. I do not, of course, mean the unconscious, automatic functions that allow your stomach to do its digesting, your lungs to do their breathing, your fingers to tie your shoes, and so forth. I mean your "mental knowledge," not just what you can consciously dredge forth on a moment's notice, but the names of people from the past if you think about them for awhile, etc. Some people characterize your long-term memory as your "world view," meaning all of your thoughts, their relations, their implications.

Short-term memory, on the other hand, is much more modest: it's only what you can keep in your conscious thoughts, which isn't very much—probably far less than you would suspect. In a now classic article, "The Magical Number Seven, Plus or Minus Two," George Miller proposes that we can keep only about seven items in our short-term memory at one time.[7]

But just what is an "item"? Miller has a nice analogy to a telegraph operator. If the operator is a beginner, just learning the Morse code, he probably hears each "dit" and each "dah" as a separate item—or, as Miller aptly terms it, as a separate "chunk." As the beginner gets better, he soon stops hearing the individual sounds and begins to hear them as words, which now become the separate chunks he can retain in his short-term memory. Perhaps later he can become good enough that some of the "dit's" and "dah's" will organize themselves into phrases for him, so that then he could hold as many as seven or so phrases as the chunks in his short-term memory.[8]

Now, suppose instead of dealing with a telegraph operator, we are dealing with a reader. We already noted that readers, in the encoding stage of the reading process, rarely encode individual letters: "h-o-r-s-e." Good thing, or they might overburden their short-term memory with every ten-letter word they came across. But like the experienced telegraph operator, efficient readers probably make chunks of words and phrases. Depending on the ability of the reader, then, and on his familiarity with the words and phrases he is reading, he can probably hold up to a dozen or so words in his short-term memory.

Figures 3 and 4 show what I mean.[9] Suppose you were asked to read some random letters. They might fill your short-term memory as shown in Figure 3:

Figure 3. Random Letters in Short-Term Memory

If you rearrange those letters, you get the word "rabbits," something that surely wouldn't fill all the slots in your short-term memory. If you were reading words, then, you might be able to fit this many in your short-term memory, as shown in Figure 4.

Figure 4. Words in Short-Term Memory

That would probably be a pretty heavy load, though, wouldn't it? That's why most researchers think five (or four or six) words might be a more realistic number than seven. Still, you can see that you can easily fit many more letters in your short-term memory if you can "chunk" them into words. The same thing happens when you can "chunk" some of the words into phrases. That's how you can fit as many as a dozen words into your short-term memory at once.

Would you like to check your own short-term memory? Frank Smith has a nice test in his book *Understanding Reading.*[10] Try memorizing the following sequence of words: memory term short in words more or dozen a hold can we.

Pretty hard, isn't it? But once you notice that the words in reverse order make a meaningful statement, you probably don't have any trouble at all. You may have made chunks of such phrases as "short-term memory" and "a dozen or more."[11]

Short-term memory and chunking will be very important concepts in many of the rest of the chapters in this book. As a quick example, consider this: most gobbledygook writers have writing habits that ask us to hold more chunks in our short-term memory than it can hold. The results? Our "computers" overload—and erase.

Long-Term Memory

I could say, simply, that in this step of the reading process, the reader integrates the information from short-term memory into his long-term memory—that he makes sense of whatever his short-term memory is holding. And that would certainly be true, but not true enough.

In fact, there is tremendous interaction between the text and the reader's long-term memory, "interaction" being the key word.[12] Often, we are not even aware of just how much we, as readers, contribute from our long-term memory—from our "world view"—to understanding a text. Here's an example that J. D. Bransford and M. K. Johnson use in their influential article.[13] Think about this sentence for a minute:

> Bill is able to come to the party tonight because his car broke down.

Pause for a moment and make sense of it.

According to Bransford and Johnson, most people who hear the sentence construe it as follows:

> Bill was originally going to leave town, but now he could not leave because his car broke down. Since he could not leave he could come to the party since the party was in town.

As Bransford and Johnson point out, this act by the readers of "creating an elaborate situation in order to understand the sentence is a far cry from merely interpreting the meanings of the phrases, 'Bill is able to come to the party tonight' and 'his car broke down.'"[14]

Just think of how many assumptions you had to make in order to understand the sample sentence, and then think how quickly your mind made those assumptions, without any conscious awareness. That's an important point to remember, for even if this model of reading seems somewhat complicated (and, believe me, it's quite simple compared to some of them), remember how marvelously quick the brain can be.

In the sample above about Bill, the reader had to create a scenario to account for the meaning. We do that all the time. In fact, we have a tremendous number of these scenarios at all levels of abstraction in our heads. The reading theorists call these "schemata" (the singular is "schema").[15] Let's look at another example, for the point is important. This one is from Thomas Trabasso.[16]

Consider this line which is probably familiar to you:

Mary had a little lamb.

You are probably running through the rest of the nursery rhyme in your mind by now, aren't you? But now consider these three possible second lines:

1. Its fleece was white as snow.
2. She spilled gravy and mint jelly on her dress.
3. The delivery was a difficult one and afterwards the vet needed a drink.

For sentence (1) you can still think about the nursery rhyme, but in (2) the lamb has now become Mary's meal, and in (3) we suddenly find out that Mary is not a little girl at all (at least, let's hope not) but is instead a sheep that has just discovered the joys of motherhood.

Trabasso points out that we bring a great deal of our long-term memory to any of the three pairs of sentences:

> Note the vast range of assumptions and knowledge that is necessary to understand these pairs of events. We need to know about nursery rhymes, ownership, pets, little girls, sheep, food, animal births, veterinarians, and alcohol.[17]

Now let's think of our old friends, the writers of gobbledygook. Too often they assume that their readers, people like you and me, have the same background, the same long-term memory, the same scenarios, the same schemata as they do. In some cases, we do have the important ones, but too often we do not, so the writing does not communicate. The trick for a writer, and it's no easy one, is to judge just which schemata his readers do and do not have. If the writer assumes too much, then he'll lose his readers. More about this later.

A Summary of the Model

We've just been through a simplified version of the reading process: The reader moves his eyes to a new spot on the page, making a fixation. There his brain seeks out something like a word or phrase and encodes it into a form the brain can use for further processing. Next, his brain turns to the mental lexicon—or dictionary—to find the meaning of the word, thus decoding it. Then the word or phrase goes into the short-term memory. At the appropriate time, the short-term memory integrates its contents with the long-term memory, thus making sense of the reading material.

A FEW REFINEMENTS

The model I've depicted so far is accurate as far as it goes, but it needs a few refinements. Let me elaborate.

Immediacy and Sentence Wrap-Up

I just mentioned that the short-term memory integrates its contents with the long-term memory "at the appropriate time." Just when is that? There are two theories, the theory of immediacy and the theory of sentence wrap-up, that at first seem contradictory but that really complement each other.

I'll start with the theory of sentence wrap-up. According to this theory, words and phrases continue to build up in the short-term memory until the reader comes to the end of a sentence. Then, with a complete and meaningful unit of thought in his short-term memory, he pauses for a few hundred milliseconds and integrates the material into his long-term memory. To check this hypothesis, Just and Carpenter examined the length of fixations at the ends of sentences. Sure enough, readers did consistently spend longer on fixations there. The same phenomenon tended to occur at the ends of clauses, too.[18]

But Just and Carpenter add a refinement to their theory of sentence wrap-up. Although many times readers wait until the ends of clauses or sentences to move information from their short-term memory to their long-term memory, sometimes they do it sooner if they can make sense of the information sooner. This is called "immediacy." According to Just and Carpenter, "Readers interpret a word while they are fixating it, and they continue to fixate it until they have processed it as far as they can."[19] Processing a single word all the way from eye fixation to the long-term memory would be unusual, of course; but the point is that readers don't necessarily have to wait until the ends of clauses or sentences. Whenever they have a sufficiently meaningful unit, integration with the long-term memory can occur (though that's often at the ends of clauses or sentences).

Let's look at an example of integration occurring after only part of a sentence:

> Although he spoke softly, yesterday's speaker could hear the little boy's question.[20]

As you're reading this sentence, you first think that the speaker is the one talking softly, don't you? That's because you've already begun to integrate the sentence in your long-term memory before you get to the end of it. As Just and Carpenter note, "The point of this example is not so much that the initial integration of 'he' and 'speaker' is incorrect, but that the integration is attempted at the earliest opportunity."[21]

According to the theory of sentence wrap-up, then, readers usually move information from their short-term memory into their long-term memory at the ends of clauses or sentences. And according to the theory of immediacy, that movement does not always have to wait until the ends of clauses and sentences, but *may* take place earlier if there's sufficient meaning in the short-term memory. As I said, the theories are really complementary.

The Short Persistence of Short-Term Memory

Most people think that they can remember quite well what they've read or heard. Actually, though, people can seldom retain exact words beyond the end of the sentence they've just read unless they consciously try to memorize it. In fact, once words move from the short-term memory into the long-term memory, the short-term memory erases; the long-term memory, therefore, tends to retain not verbatim material but rather the broader meaning.

Goldman et al. conducted an experiment that made two interesting points: first, people have trouble remembering the words they read in the immediately previous sentence once they've started the next one; second, if a sentence is long, people reading the end of it can't remember the exact words at the beginning of it.[22] In other words, the short-term memory doesn't hold very much information, and it doesn't hold it very long.

Let me describe the experiment. Goldman had some grade school students read stories that had only about 20-30 words on a page. But sometimes the students were surprised when they turned the page. Instead of seeing some more of the story, they saw only a single word. Actually, this was a word from the page they had just finished. Without looking back at that page, the students had to try to remember what word had *followed* the word they were now looking at.

Let me give you a quick example. Suppose that what you are reading now, this paragraph, is like the story the students read. If you turned the page now and saw only a single word—"what"—could you tell me the word that followed it in this paragraph? Think for a moment.

The right answer is "you." I'm simplifying a little, but Goldman found that, by a significant margin, students could usually recall the word if it occurred in the sentence they were still reading. But if they had already started another sentence, then they often couldn't remember a word from the sentence they had just finished. This is consistent with the theory that the short-term memory tends to erase after starting new clauses or sentences.

Also, if the word was fairly far back in the same sentence, the students had trouble remembering it. This is consistent with the theory that the short-term memory can hold only a limited number of chunks before it erases.

The same pattern of results occurred in a second experiment by Goldman et al. involving not just grade school students but also adults.[23]

Automaticity

Even though there are some limitations, the model I've presented so far requires a very sophisticated processing mechanism, which the human brain is. Yet we know we sometimes have trouble keeping our attention fixed on any task for very long. How, then, can we possibly do something as complicated as this model makes reading appear to be? The answer, in a long word, is "automaticity."[24]

The answer, in other words, is that we do not actually have our *attention* on all of those steps in the process. Ideally, our attention should be on the integrating stage in which we move information into our long-term memory. The rest of the process should be

automatic. But we do not live in an ideal world, so that is not always the case. Children learning to read, for example, often do not
easily recognize words, so their attention shifts from the integrating step to the step where the brain consults the mental lexicon.
Shifts of attention like that can cause the reading process to slow
down or even to break down entirely for the moment.

Children are not the only ones who have to shift their attention away from the integrating step—we all have that happen on
every page we read. And if we're reading gobbledygook, it happens
far more often than once or twice a page. We'll come back to
automaticity throughout the rest of the book, for the gobbledygook
writer is very skilled at diverting attention from where we, the
readers, would like it to be.

Interaction

Probably the first thing a reading theorist would notice about this
chapter is that I have made the flow seem entirely in one direction
—from fixations on the reading material to encoding to the mental
lexicon to the short-term memory to the long-term memory. That
is actually an oversimplification.

The model I have presented so far is what the theorists would
call "bottom up," meaning that information flows only toward the
long-term memory. Most theorists today, however, believe that the
process is more accurately a combination of "bottom up" and "top
down." That is, not only does information flow from a fixation all
the way to the long-term memory, but it can also flow from the
long-term memory back in the other direction. That way, the long-
term memory can help out with other parts of the reading process.[25]

For example, suppose that the long-term memory learns that
the subject of the reading material is baseball. That information
can then flow from the top down to other parts of the process.
Then if the mental lexicon needs to search for the word "strike," it
can select the meaning pertaining to baseball immediately and ignore meanings pertaining to union activities or to violent blows.

In fact, simply showing that information flows from eye fixations to the long-term memory, and also from the long-term memory back the other way, would still not be sufficient. Using short-
cuts and by-passes, the brain sends information directly where it

is needed without flowing through unnecessary parts of the process. This kind of interaction makes reading much more efficient.

A LIMITED-CAPACITY PROCESSOR

Now for the final point, but an important one, indeed: the brain is a limited capacity processor. As marvelous as it is and as easily, as almost effortlessly, as it can handle the complex process of moving information from some black marks on a piece of paper into information in the long-term memory, it can do only so much. Donald Foss and David Hakes have a nice analogy in their college text:

> Imagine yourself driving down a freeway on a clear day with no traffic. It would be possible to play a game of mental tic-tac-toe with your passenger, and the game would go relatively quickly. Now imagine that the traffic is nearly bumper-to-bumper at 55 mph and that it is dark and rainy out. It would probably not occur to you to play mental anything at that point (at least we hope not). However, if you did decide to play mental tic-tac-toe, then the time that you would take for each move would be longer than under good driving conditions.[26]

When you're reading gobbledygook, you suddenly find yourself on that dark and rainy road fighting bumper-to-bumper traffic. Your brain is struggling with difficult reading conditions. The rest of the book will offer some help so that your readers don't find themselves in such a predicament.

Notes for Chapter 4

1.   Donald J. Foss and David T. Hakes, *Psycholinguistics: An Introduction to the Psychology of Language* (Englewood Cliffs, N.J.: Prentice-Hall, 1978), pp. 325-27.

2.   Marcel Adam Just and Patricia A. Carpenter, "A Theory of Reading: From Eye Fixations to Comprehension," *Psychological Review,* 87, No. 4 (1980), 330.

3.   Foss and Hakes, pp. 329-42. This is a fascinating discussion, if you are into this sort of thing, of the various possibilities for encoding. The authors offer three possibilities: the subvocalization hypothesis, the direct access hypothesis,

and the phonological recoding hypothesis. Then, with admirable temerity, they opt for a fourth: the dual access hypothesis.

The subvocalization hypothesis says that readers actually convert reading into subvocal speech, even asserting that readers move such speech muscles as their larynx and lips. One experiment actually supports such muscle movement, though Foss and Hakes imply that such an experiment was an anomaly. One compelling bit of evidence against this hypothesis is that we can't talk any faster than about five syllables a second. Since we shouldn't be able to read any faster than we talk—according to this hypothesis—the maximum reading rate would be no more than 300 words per minute *if* all the words were monosyllables (p. 331).

The direct access hypothesis says that readers can go directly from the printed representation of a word to the mental lexicon—that there is no recoding. Frank Smith, in *Understanding Reading*, is a strong advocate of this position. There is some evidence for this position in experiments cited by Foss and Hakes.

The third, the phonological recoding hypothesis, says that readers convert words to a phonological code specific to reading, related perhaps only to phonemes but probably including affixes as separate entities. This phonological recoding does not happen at the stage where the speech muscles can become involved, as in the subvocalization hypothesis, but later.

Foss and Hakes present some interesting experiments to support and refute both of these last two hypotheses. As a result, they say that both are probably right to some extent. That's where the fourth option—the dual access hypothesis—comes from.

4. Frank Smith, *Understanding Reading: A Psycholinguistic Analysis of Reading and Learning to Read,* 2 ed. (New York: Holt, Rinehart, and Winston, 1978), p. 208.

5. Don L. Scarborough, Charles Cortese, and Hollis S. Scarborough, "Frequency and Repetition Effects in Lexical Memory," *Journal of Experimental Psychology: Human Perception and Performance,* 3, No. 1 (1977). This is the key study on word frequency. However, other experiments looking at other aspects of the reading process often use word frequency as one of the variables. Consistently, word frequency is a significant factor: the lower the frequency of a word, the longer the reader takes to process it. In the Just and Carpenter article, for example, which measured the time of each eye fixation, the times were consistently longer for words of lower frequency (that is, for less common words).

I might add here that the standard source for word frequency these days is *Computational Analysis of Present-Day American English* by Henry Kucera and W. Nelson Francis (Providence, R.I.: Brown University Press, 1967). This book, obviously with the help of a computer, lists word frequencies found in over a million words of text selected as representative. I'll be referring to this book again.

6. Just and Carpenter, pp. 338-41.

7. George A. Miller, "The Magical Number Seven, Plus or Minus Two: Some Limits on Our Capacity for Processing Information," *The Psychology Review,*

63, No. 2 (1956), 90-95. This is a classic, well worth reading. Miller's emphasis is on perception, not comprehension, so he shows that people have difficulty distinguishing among seven or so different sound pitches, loudnesses, taste intensities, color hues, and much more—no matter how narrow or how broad the range. So if you hear a number of sounds within a narrow range of pitch, or within a broad range, you still won't be able to distinguish more than about seven (roughly) different pitches. Miller turns from perception to comprehension at the end of the article, and introduces the term "chunking." He originated the term.

8.   Miller, p. 93. If you're interested in a philosophical discussion of what a composite—or a "chunk"—is, you might like to see Ludwig Wittgenstein's *Philosophical Investigations I*, Section 47. It's not totally relevant here, but it is fun. You'll never quite be sure what composite means any more.

9.   I remember seeing a similar illustration somewhere. I have searched, but I cannot find the source.

10.   Smith, p. 53.

11.   Of course, we are only guessing when we try to determine exactly how the chunking takes place. Frank Smith emphasizes that "it is not the sequence of a dozen or so words that we are holding in short-term memory, but rather their meaning" (p. 53).

12.   This is a common notion today, assumed in Just and Carpenter, cited above, and in Rumelhart, cited below.

13.   John D. Bransford and Marcia K. Johnson, "Considerations of Some Problems of Comprehension," in *Visual Information Processing*, ed. William G. Chase (New York: Academic Press, 1973), p. 391. This article is another classic, especially important on the role of the reader in making inferences. It contains a profusion of examples.

14.   Bransford and Johnson, p. 391.

15.   I was introduced to the concept in David E. Rumelhart's article, "Schemata: The Building Blocks of Cognition," in *Comprehension and Teaching: Research Reviews*, ed. John T. Guthrie (Newark, Delaware: International Reading Association, 1981), pp. 3-26. See also an article by Marilyn Jager Adams and Allan Collins, "A Schema-Theoretic View of Reading," in *New Directions in Discourse Processing*, Vol. 2, ed. Roy O. Freedle (Norwood, N.J.: Ablex, 1979). The Rumelhart article is especially readable and especially good. If there's one part of the reading process that I under-emphasize in this chapter, it's the contribution of schemata to reading. Adequate treatment would have to be lengthy, however, too lengthy for the purposes it would serve later in this book.

16.   Thomas Trabasso, "On the Making of Inferences During Reading and Their Assessment," in *Comprehension and Teaching*, cited above, pp. 59-60.

17.   Trabasso, p. 60.

18.   Just and Carpenter, p. 346.

19.   Just and Carpenter, p. 350.

20.   Just and Carpenter, p. 343.

21.   Just and Carpenter, p. 343.

22.   Susan R. Goldman, et al., "Short-Term Retention of Discourse During Reading," *Journal of Educational Psychology,* 72, No. 5 (1980), 647-55.

23.   Goldman, pp. 652-54.

24.   David LaBerge and S. Jay Samuels, "Toward a Theory of Automatic Information Processing in Reading," *Cognitive Psychology,* 6 (1974), 293-323. This is another of the classic articles on reading theory, cited frequently in more recent work.

25.   The Rumelhart article, already cited, has an especially good example of interactivity, pp. 16-19.

26.   Foss and Hakes, p. 106.

B   A New Style

5 WRITE INFORMALLY

So far, we've been theoretical, examining some misconceptions about writing and discussing contemporary models for the reading and writing processes. This part of the book is primarily practical: Just what should you do to make your writing easier for others to read? And just what should you do to make your writing easier for you to write?

The most general recommendation I have is for you to write the way you talk. I know that sounds too simple, and if you're suspicious of such advice, I suspect you've read some of the simplistic books I have read. Yet bear with me, because I think the advice is important if we qualify what we mean by "talk." So think of this recommendation, for the moment, only as a general guideline.

Still, even people who decide to write the way they talk often don't know what to do next. What specific features of talking should they transfer to their writing? I've organized my advice into these five categories, with a chapter on each of them:

1. Use simple words (Chapter 6).
2. Use a natural word order (Chapter 7).
3. Don't overdo conciseness (Chapter 8).

4. Give the reader "road signs" (Chapter 9).
5. Be careful with your sentence structure (Chapter 10).

Except for the third category, "Don't overdo conciseness," my advice appears rather traditional. But some interesting things will happen as we get more specific.

WRITE THE WAY YOU TALK

For the rest of the chapter, let's consider my most general advice, that you should write the way you talk.

In my model of writing in Chapter 3, I emphasized the importance of finding your voice, of discovering or creating a personality that could help you write more easily and more clearly. If you think for a moment, you will probably agree that you are most "yourself" when you are in an informal situation; everything you do seems more natural. For example, you can probably speak more easily when you're having a friendly talk with a companion you trust. The same goes for writing: you can write more easily, more naturally, if you feel at ease. One way of doing that is to imagine, when you are writing, that you are having a friendly conversation with someone. Then "say the words" on paper as you would say them to that friend.

You may object that such writing might be too informal, that it might tend to be so chatty or cute that it would offend. Well, then you must adjust your imagination. Don't imagine shooting the breeze with a friend in a bar, but perhaps imagine talking with a fairly new acquaintance you think you're going to like. I once heard a U.S. Senator urge his staff members to answer his mail as though they were writing to a distant aunt or uncle.

There's no need, in other words, to violate the psychological space that you and your reader might wish to have between you. You don't need to slap strangers on the back—just try to be friendly, informal, easy.

If you've read anything about clear writing, or if you've taken any courses in it, the advice to write the way you talk is probably familiar to you. Specialists in the field have been giving such advice for years. Here, from several books and one article, are some excerpts that I consider particularly well stated:

If only you were here I could *say* all this to you!

> —Walker Gibson discussing the attitude a writer
> should have toward his reader, *The Limits of Lan-*
> *guage,* 1962[1]

When you catch yourself writing a vague or complex phrase
or sentence, ask yourself:
"How would I *say* that? If the reader were sitting across the
desk how would I say it to him? What would I tell him if he
were on the other end of a long-distance wire?"

> —Robert Gunning, *The Technique of Clear Writing,*
> 1968[2]

Many of my students have found it helpful to use other little
mental aids. The trick is to remind yourself of talk in a conversational tone, in informal surroundings. Try to imagine yourself talking about *this* subject to *this* person at lunch, across a
cafeteria or restaurant table. Punctuate your sentences, in
your mind, with a gulp of coffee or a bite from a sandwich. In-
tersperse your thoughts mentally with an occasional "you
know" or just simply "Joe." Can you say "If there are additional
infractions, Joe, we shall have no alternative but to request that
you make other banking arrangements"? Of course you can't.
So write as you talk. Talk, talk, talk on paper. Go over what
you've written and try to listen to it. Does it sound like talk? If
not, change it until it does.

> —Rudolf Flesch, *On Business Communications,* 1972[3]

The two best ways I know of promoting an authentic and
readable style are these:
1. Write with the assumption that your reader is a compan-
ionable friend with a warm sense of humor and an apprecia-
tion of simple straightforwardness.
2. Write as if you were actually talking to that friend, but
talking with enough leisure to frame your thoughts concisely
and interestingly.

> —John Trimble, *Writing with Style,* 1975[4]

Writing which is much closer to talk than most school writing is at present should be encouraged right through the
child's years at school—and across the whole curriculum. We

believe that such writing would free the writer to think in writing and to learn through using written language in the same way that he already uses talk.

—Nancy Martin, et al., *Writing and Learning across the Curriculum 11-16,* 1976[5]

Your writing as a manager goes to your subordinates, your colleagues and your superiors. If your memos and business letters make you sound like a pompous illiterate, they may make you the laughingstock of the office.

To avoid this, a useful way to revise your business writing is called the Conversation Test. As you revise, ask yourself if you would ever say to your reader what you are writing. Or imagine yourself speaking to the person instead of writing. If you were talking to a business colleague, would you ever say: "In response to your memo of 11/18/81"? If you did, he would probably laugh.

If you were speaking to a customer, would you ever say: "Enclosed please find your order for three (3) replacement keys"? If you did, your customer would surely think you were weird.

—John Louis DiGaetani, *Wall Street Journal,* 1982[6]

Most of these writers tell you to picture yourself in a specific situation, that by doing so you can learn to write clearly. If you'll recall, that is exactly what I stumbled upon when I was writing my first book. The words finally came easily when I pictured myself talking to my class, people I was comfortable with. Without knowing it, I began to "write the way I talked."

There are, of course, significant differences between writing and talking, some of which make writing easier than talking and some of which make it harder. Let's discuss those differences briefly, and then turn to the similarities between good informal writing and good informal talking.

DIFFERENCES BETWEEN WRITING AND TALKING

A Russian psychologist, Lev Vygotsky, saw writing as a far more abstract mental process than talking. A child learning to write, for instance, must "disengage himself from the sensory aspect of speech and replace words by images of words."[7] That is, the words in speech are physically *said*, but in writing the words must be *imagined*. Then the words go down on paper. Learning to write, then, according to Vygotsky, "naturally must be as much harder than oral speech for the child as algebra is harder than arithmetic."[8] Vygotsky's point is rather abstract, yet there are other, more easily discernible differences between writing and talking.

One difference is that when people talk there is usually some interaction as the conversation takes place. The listener, for example, might make these responses as you're trying to tell him about something: "Oh, I see." "What do you mean by that?" "Hmmm." The writer, on the other hand, doesn't have the advantage of such feedback. All he has in front of him is a sheet of paper. At best, he can attempt to get some feedback by later showing someone what he wrote. However, that is quite a bit different from the interaction of a face-to-face talk, with all of its give and take.

Another difference is that speakers use their tone of voice and body gestures—such as pointing—as additional means of communication. For instance, you can say the word "okay" so that it clearly communicates reluctance, anger, boredom, or eagerness. But there's no tone to the bare word "okay" on a printed page. A writer would have to signify reluctance or eagerness with more words.

So far, we've discussed only the differences between speaking and writing that place speaking at an advantage. But writing has its advantages, too.

Let's think in terms of our simplified model of the writing process: prewriting, writing, and rewriting. When you're getting ready to write something, in the prewriting stage, you can take all the time you wish to prepare, but when you're speaking—particularly in conversation—you rarely have such an advantage. Even if you think you're prepared, the interaction—the give-and-take of conversation —can move you in unexpected directions.

At the next stage, during the actual writing, as a writer you can pause silently—even in the middle of a sentence—as you plan what to put down next. But when you're having a conversation, such pauses can be embarrassing. Speakers tend to fill them with "ums" and "you knows." Or they just keep talking, using whatever words and ideas come to mind.

During the final stage, the rewriting, as a writer you can edit your draft, getting everything right before the reader sees it. But as a speaker, you must "show" your listener your first draft.

These are some of the important differences between writing and talking, the ones we can't do much about. Now let's turn to some similarities, not between writing and talking, though, but between *good* informal writing and *good* informal talking.

THE SIMILARITIES OF INFORMAL
WRITING AND INFORMAL TALKING

When do you think you're at your best as a talker? When you're standing on a stage before a thousand people or when you're talking in your backyard with a friend? I think most of us would agree that we can talk better when we're in the relaxed cirumstance, such as the talk with a friend.

The same applies to writing. Once you make the breakthrough to writing informally, the way you talk, you will find it is much easier to do your best writing. In fact, you will never want to write any other way.

You may object that there are certain circumstances when you have to stand before large groups and talk, whether you want to or not. In fact, you may say, government, military, business, and academic writing is more analogous to the formal situation before an audience than to the informal situation in your backyard. Should you act before the large audience the way you would act with a friend?

Yes, of course. Think about yourself for a moment not as a speaker but as a listener. Which speakers, on public occasions, give the best speeches? The ones who are formal and frozen on stage, projecting to a faceless audience? Or the ones who are relaxed, informal up there, speaking naturally, quietly, and easily?

The good platform speakers have learned to talk before audiences the same way they would talk before friends. In a way, they have learned to "talk" (before large groups) the way they talk (with friends).

What, then, are some of the similarities between good informal talking and good informal writing?

First, both have some important similarities in language patterns: the words are usually simpler, the subjects and verbs usually come early in the sentences (speakers usually can't think far enough ahead to do otherwise), and so forth. Once you can "plug into" informal writing, then, the change to an informal language pattern will make your writing clearer and easier to read (just as an informal speaker before large groups is easier to listen to).

A second similarity is that both informal speaking and informal writing seem to issue from the same personality, the same role. Almost all of us have found our voices as informal speakers; virtually all of us have a relaxed, informal personality (at least somewhere, sometime) with a relaxed informal voice for speaking. That same voice can produce good public speaking (learning to "talk" the way you talk, as I said) and good "public" writing.

You already have the "voice" or role you need, in other words. You just need to learn to apply it to your writing. Then the words and ideas will come both more easily and more clearly.

AN EXPERIMENT

The next time you have something to write, especially something simple like a memo or a short letter, try this: imagine yourself face-to-face with the person you're writing to. What would you say if you were *telling* him your message? Then write down the words you would actually say. Don't worry. You don't have to show this to anyone (yet). Think of your draft as a private experiment.

Next, use the advantage of being a writer instead of being a speaker to edit what you've said. But be careful; don't translate your spoken words back to the usual writing. Just edit for preciseness. Let the language stay simple.

You may be surprised at how hard it is for you to make yourself write even a private draft of spoken language. But you'd probably be even more surprised at how few people will notice the specific differences between your "spoken" writing and your old style. They'll just notice the good effect.

The next step is obvious. After you've edited your draft, get it typed and send it. Then keep on writing that way. The rest of the book will help show you how.

Notes for Chapter 5

1. Walker Gibson, *The Limits of Language* (New York: Hill and Wang, 1962), p. 105. I consider Gibson's style a model of good writing. His book *Tough, Sweet & Stuffy* (Bloomington, Indiana: Indiana University Press, 1966) is a perceptive and entertaining examination of three different "voices" that Gibson finds in writing.

2. Robert Gunning, *The Technique of Clear Writing*, rev. ed. (New York: McGraw-Hill, 1968), p. 120.

3. Rudolph Flesch, *On Business Communications: How to Say What You Mean in Plain English* (New York: Barnes and Noble, 1972), p. 11. Like Gunning's book, this one is also an outdated classic. Yet Flesch gives his advice to write informally so forcefully and so persuasively that it's worth reading. By the way, the hardcover title is much less stodgy: *Say What You Mean.*

4. John Trimble, *Writing with Style: Conversations on the Art of Writing* (Englewood Cliffs, N.J.: Prentice-Hall, 1975), p. 77. Chapter 8 of this book, "Tips for Increasing Your Readability," is well worth reading. Trimble's style is excellent.

5. Nancy Martin, et al., *Writing and Learning across the Curriculum 11-16*, Schools Council Writing across the Curriculum Project, University of London Institute of Education (London: Hollen Street Press, 1976), p. 61. Although this book reports on writing conditions in England, many English teachers in this country find it very much applicable here.

6. John Louis DiGaetani, "Conversation: The Key to Better Business Writing," *Wall Street Journal*, February 8, 1982.

7. Lev Vygotsky, *Thought and Language*, ed. and trans. Eugenia Hanfmann and Gertrude Vakar (Cambridge, Mass.: The M.I.T. Press, 1962), p. 98.

8. Vygotsky, p. 99.

6   USE SIMPLE WORDS

If you have heard only one bit of advice for making writing easier to read, it is probably to use simple words—or short words or common words or Anglo-Saxon words (whichever ones they are).

Yet, clearly, many people who hear that advice also ignore it. Why? When I ignored it, I felt that as long as I knew the meaning of a word—or as long as I could expect my reader to know it—then why not use it? We are, after all, educated and intelligent people, are we not? Since I know the meanings of both "commence" and "begin," is there any reason I should prefer one over the other?

I didn't think so, but I was wrong. Experiments show convincingly that even intelligent, educated, and skilled readers have more trouble with relatively uncommon words—like "commence" —than they do with relatively common ones—like "begin." Imagine what happens when those same readers encounter not just one relatively uncommon word but sentences, paragraphs, and pages of them. And then imagine what happens when the uncommon words aren't the only problem with the writing, when the sentence structures, etc., also tax the reader's finite capabilities.

Now, before I begin, let me offer a qualification. Even two words that we consider synonyms, such as "commence" and "begin," do not mean *exactly* the same thing. There are nuances of meaning that distinguish them. Even if we don't consider the context, sometimes these nuances—or "connotations"—are obvious and important. "Chubby" and "fat" both mean overweight, but the first word seems to be forgiving whereas the second would more likely be condemning. The words are synonyms, but their connotations certainly distinguish them.

As I'm sure you noticed, the title of this chapter urges you to "use simple words." Of course I don't want you to say "fat" instead of "chubby" or "bulky" or "swollen" if those words seem to have just the right nuance of meaning. On the other hand, don't say "corporeally substantial" if all you mean is "fat."

I'm sure you've noticed that the problem with gobbledygook writers is not that they seem overly careful of nuances of meaning.

Or perhaps they are, but the nuance has to do with defining *themselves* as "impressive" people and not the nuances of the meaning of their material. Let me explain.

Gobbledygook writers often systematically select the impressive word over the simpler one every time. "Corporeally substantial" has an impressive quality to it that "fat" does not. The nuance that gobbledygook writers are after, then, is that of impressiveness. But the flaw is that the nuance does not apply to the subject (to the overweight person) but to the *writer*.

As you read this chapter, then, remember that I do not ask you to ignore the subtle meanings in words. But I do ask you not to systematically choose words, at the expense of your readers, just to puff yourself up. That tactic backfires with alert readers, anyway. And I also ask you, when the nuances between two words are insubstantial in your judgment, to systematically choose the simpler one.

The rest of this chapter will explain why.

WORD FREQUENCY

Researchers have settled on a number of factors that can make a word easier to read: we spend less time reading words with fewer syllables, words we first learned while we were young, and words that are relatively unfamiliar to us but that we have been reminded of fairly recently.[1] However, the most important factor is a word's frequency. Just how often have we come across a word? The more often we have seen it—the higher its frequency—the easier it is for us to read.

For dealing with word frequency, most researchers today rely on a computer analysis that Henry Kucera and W. Nelson Francis published in 1967. Kucera and Francis examined over a million words of printed material, and list the frequency of various words.[2] What do you suppose the most frequent word in English is? I'll list the top twenty-five, along with the number of occurrences per million words of text:

1.	the	69,971	14.	as	7,250
2.	of	36,411	15.	his	6,997
3.	and	28,582	16.	on	6,742
4.	to	26,149	17.	be	6,377
5.	a	23,237	18.	at	5,378
6.	in	21,341	19.	by	5,305
7.	that	10,595	20.	I	5,173
8.	is	10,099	21.	this	5,146
9.	was	9,816	22.	had	5,133
10.	he	9,543	23.	not	4,609
11.	for	9,489	24.	are	4,393
12.	it	8,756	25.	but	4,381
13.	with	7,289			

As you can see, the frequent words are also short. In fact, if you could see Kucera and Francis' entire list, you would notice that very frequent words tend to have only one or two syllables, while less frequent ones tend to have three or more. Still, we cannot accept word length as the primary guide to reading ease because some very short words are also very infrequent. The word "grig," for instance, meaning "grasshopper," has only one syllable and four letters, yet it's so infrequent that it isn't even on Kucera and Francis' list.

The central criterion for readability, then, is a word's frequency. Let's turn now to a couple of experiments—and there are many—that prove the point.

Scarborough, Cortese, and Scarborough

In 1977, Scarborough, Cortese, and Scarborough published an article on the processing time for words of different frequencies.[3] They asked college students to look at individual groupings of four letters. Some of these groups of letters spelled high-frequency words, some low-frequency words, and some just pronounceable non-words. The students would then look at one of the letter groupings and try to determine as quickly as possible if it spelled a word or if it didn't. They would press one button to respond to words, another for non-words.

Researchers theorized that the students should be able to find the high-frequency (common) words more quickly in their mental dictionaries, and thus press the button quickly. They would be slower to press the button for the low-frequency words, and slowest of all for the non-words, having to run through much more of their mental dictionaries before eliminating them.

The results? As expected, the students pressed the buttons significantly faster for the high-frequency words, slower for the low-frequency words, and slowest of all for the non-words.

Such results are typical. If there's one result that shows up consistently in the different experiments that researchers conduct, it is that readers take longer to identify low-frequency words.

But what happens when people are actually reading instead of participating in something artificial like recognizing words from lists?

Just and Carpenter

In Chapter 4 I told you about Just and Carpenter's experiment using a television camera to record eye fixations while students actually read material. Just and Carpenter checked to see if the students had longer eye fixations for low-frequency (uncommon) words. As expected, the students did pause longer on those words.[4]

Think about the implications for your writing. Lower frequency words—just single instances of them—are more demanding of your reader.

Now, the cameras didn't show much absolute difference—only an average of 53 milliseconds for each factor of 10 in word frequency. However, the difference is consistent and much more significant than that small amount of time seems to indicate. Let me explain, for the point is an important one.

At the end of Chapter 4, I said that the brain is a limited capacity processor; it can do only so much at one time. I also quoted an analogy to someone trying to play mental tic-tac-toe while driving. There's no problem when traffic is light and the weather is good, but there are big problems during rush hour on a rainy evening: the driving or (more likely) the mental tic-tac-toe will go.

The same occurs in reading. When we come across a difficult word, we have to spend more time to look it up in our mental dictionary. During that time, other processing, such as making sense of the material in the long-term memory, almost certainly suffers. So the extra processing time for uncommon words is just an indicator of other important problems in the reading process. After 53 milliseconds on a tougher word, you may have looked up that word in your mental dictionary, but you've probably lost some understanding elsewhere at the same time.

And, once again, imagine what happens when you are confronted not just by a single difficult word but by many of them.

Another Experiment

You might wish to try an experiment on yourself. The following two passages are as alike as possible in structure, but one version uses relatively easy words and the other relatively difficult ones, though you surely have seen these "difficult" words many times. Yet notice that the passage with the more difficult words is still probably harder for you to understand, even after reading the easier passage just before it:

Easy Passage

In the forest there was a watering hole. The animals who had helped in digging the hole were all allowed to drink from it. But the lazy jackal, who had not helped, used to come early in the morning and drink until full. When the other animals realized that someone was stealing their water, they were very angry.

Hard Passage

In the forest there was a watering hole. The animals who had rendered assistance in digging the hole were, without exception, granted permission to imbibe from it. However, the indolent jackal, who had not assisted, was wont to come early in the morning and imbibe until satisfied. When the remaining animals became cognizant that someone was pilfering the water, they were extremely angry.[5]

These paragraphs were part of an experiment that Douglas Vipond ran on college students. There were several different passages, each with a hard and an easy version, so some students would read a hard version of one passage and an easy version of another; they didn't all read two versions of the same passage as I asked you to do.

The students had enough time to read the passages, but not enough time to study them. Afterwards, they were asked to recall as much as they could. As you can guess, the students did significantly better recalling the easy passages. Interestingly, Vipond had already categorized the students by reading ability. Both the skilled and the less skilled readers did significantly better on the easy passages.[6]

A Theory

Why do people get into the habit of systematically choosing hard words over easy ones? One culprit may be a usage scale that was once popular in English textbooks. Usually these scales are preceded by a list of "formal" words and their "informal" equivalents, such as this list:[7]

Formal	*Informal*
accompany	go with
assist	help
locate	find
participate	take part
subsequent	later (etc.)

Then the books present a usage scale showing when people should use the formal words and when they should use the informal equivalents. Here's such a scale, adapted from a still-popular college text on business writing:[8]

Levels of Language	Uses
Formal	Doctoral dissertations
	Master's theses
	Legal documents
	Top-level government agreements and papers
Informal	Business letters
	Business reports
	Newspapers
	Magazine articles
	Bulletins
	Manuals
	House publications
Substandard	Not acceptable

See the problem? With "formal" at the top and "substandard" at the bottom, the scale seems to go from good to bad. Where does that leave the informal words? The implication is certainly that the informal words are only all right, that the formal words are really the best language. Even though the scale seems to show that informal language is appropriate for business matters, the implication is that formal language might really be better, perhaps safer. The underlying message is to use "anticipate," "ascertain," and "conflagration" instead of their simpler equivalents.

That message can cause people to systematically choose the harder rather than the easier words. You have already seen the damage that can do to the reading process.

The real question is whether people should ever systematically choose the formal words. Is there really a need, as the scale explicitly says, to use such language for academic, legal, and governmental writing? No. Not if we take into account contemporary reading theory.

My objection, then, is to the usage scale above, not to the list of formal and informal words that preceded it. In fact, I like such a

list. I would just apply it differently. Instead of recommending that
you use the formal words on certain occasions and informal words
on others, I'd recommend that you do away with the formal words.
Or use them sparingly if their connotations demand it. Certainly,
though, don't prefer the formal words systematically as most gobbledygook writers do.

Breaking the Habit

Since contemporary reading theory shows that even single instances of less common words place a greater strain on our readers, I suggest that you examine your writing to see where you can
make substitutions. I did the same thing once.

Not long after I wrote that textbook that I mentioned, I moved
to Washington, D.C., where I spent three years in a bureaucratic
writing job. As I tried to apply the lessons I had learned from writing the text, I was amazed and distressed to see that I, too, had
been tricked by the underlying message of the usage scale. I had
been systematically choosing the more "impressive" formal words.
I set about to eliminate them wherever possible. With practice, I
learned to systematically choose the easier version unless I had a
good reason not to. The formal words slowly became the exception
rather than the rule.

I suggest you examine your writing in the same way I once
did. Let the hard words be red flags to you.

Below is a list of some difficult words and the simpler substitutions you can make for them.[9] The list could be much longer
and still not cover many of the offenders.

Difficult	Simpler
accompany	go with
accomplish	do
advise	tell, recommend
afford an opportunity	allow, let
anticipate	expect
approximately	about
assist	help
attached herewith is	here's

at the present time	now
close proximity	near
commence	begin
conclude	end
concur	agree
cooperate	help
demonstrate	prove, show
effect	make
endeavor	try
exhibit	show
facilitate	help
failed to	didn't
forward	send
has the capability	can
identical	same
incumbent upon	must
indicate	show, write down
initial	first
locate	find
maintain	keep, support
modify	change
notify	let me know, tell
participate	take part
permit	let
prior to	before
provided that	if
purchase	buy
relating to	about, on
request	ask
retain	keep
state	say
subsequent	later, next
sufficient	enough
terminate	stop
transpire	happen
utilize, utilization	use
witnessed	saw

You may wonder if there is ever an occasion to use words of low frequency. Absolutely. For one thing, not all words have easy and hard versions like "begin" and "commence." What, for example, are simple synonyms for "trowel" or "relegate"? If you need a low frequency word for its preciseness, and you think it's in your reader's vocabulary, then don't even hesitate to use it.

Sometimes you're justified in using the hard version of a pair of words if the hard version seems to carry the right connotation. Consider, for example, the words "pretentious" and "showy," which are essentially synonymous. If you're trying to describe a red-neck in a country and western bar doing the Cotton Eye Joe dance, however, you'd hardly choose the word "pretentious"; it connotes a kind of showiness that has to do with overinflated dignity that the red-neck and the Cotton Eye Joe do not.

The main point, then, is not to reach continuously and systematically for the harder word without a reason. Don't reach for "utilize" when all you mean to say is "use."[10] Prefer the simple word, not the hard one.

Let me give you an example of a writer who seems to choose the simple word over the hard one, yet who is also an acknowledged master of the English language: E.B. White. I'll quote a passage from his famous introduction to his book on writing, *The Elements of Style*. White was updating the book for his deceased friend and former teacher, Will Strunk. As you read White's entertaining description of Will Strunk in the introduction to the book, notice how ordinary most of the words are; and notice also how extraordinary the effect is. No gobbledygook here. No effort to impress. No concern with choosing formal words. There is only a concern for choosing the *right* words —precise, colorful, and wonderfully apt words:

> "Omit needless words!" cries the author on page 23, and into that imperative Will Strunk really put his heart and soul. In the days when I was sitting in his class, he omitted so many words, and omitted them so forcibly and with such eagerness and obvious relish, that he often seemed in the position of having shortchanged himself—a man left with nothing more to say yet with time to fill, a radio prophet who had outdistanced the clock. Will Strunk got out of his predicament by a

simple trick: he uttered every sentence three times. When he delivered his oration on brevity to the class, he leaned forward over his desk, grasped his coat lapels in his hands, and, in a husky, conspiratorial voice, said, "Rule Seventeen. Omit needless words! Omit needless words! Omit needless words!"[11]

Beautiful writing, isn't it? I once checked this passage against the Dale-Chall list of the 3000 familiar words that 80 percent of fourth graders know.[12] Would you believe that 84 percent of the words from this passage are on the fourth grade list? Yet White is one of the greatest essayists in English in the twentieth century. When he chooses a relatively uncommon word—"imperative," "predicament," "brevity"—the word fits. It's not there because it's impressive or because it's formal. It's there because it's *right*—and it's right only for a handful of occasions.

My advice, then, is for you to choose the simple word unless you have a good reason to do otherwise (and the number of times you have a good reason will probably be small). Let E.B. White's style of writing be your guide.

ABSTRACT AND CONCRETE WORDS

The words "concrete" and "abstract" are relative terms. Essentially, a word is concrete if it stands for something that is a thing, something that exists or could exist in time and space, such as an arrow or an elephant. An abstract word, on the other hand, stands for a concept, such as the words "delirium" or "necessity."[13]

One useful way to distinguish abstract and concrete words is the "ladder of abstraction": at the top of the ladder are the abstract words and phrases; at the bottom are the concrete ones. (Though, of course, some words, like "delirium," won't fit neatly on such a ladder).

Means of Transportation

Vehicles

Automobiles

Sports Cars

Mazda RX-7's

The research isn't absolutely clear in this area, but the consensus is that people in fact have more difficulty reading abstract words. Allan Paivio and Kalman Csapo, for example, published the results of an interesting experiment in 1973. They showed people brief glimpses (1/16 second) of a picture, a concrete word, or an abstract word. The people then had the rest of a 5-second interval to make notes on what they saw. Five minutes after going through a number of these episodes, the people took a test asking them to recall the pictures or words they had seen. By a significant margin, they recalled the pictures better than the words. And also by a significant margin, they recalled the concrete words better than the abstract words. It seems that people can recall material better if they can create an image of it—such as with a picture or a concrete word.[14]

A more recent experiment by Susan Belmore, et al., compared not just concrete and abstract words but concrete and abstract sentences:

Concrete: The drain of the bathtub was clogged up with hair.

Abstract: The energy of the people was used up by war.

The students participating in the experiment would see a number of experimental sentences, some concrete and some abstract. After seeing an experimental sentence, the students would then be shown a test sentence and asked to decide whether it was "probably true" or "probably false" based on the experimental sentence. For instance, after sentence "E" below, they'd be asked if sentence "T" was probably true or probably false:

E: The drain of the bathtub was filled with hair.

T: The hair clogged up the drain of the bathtub. (Probably true)

By a significant margin, and in a number of variations of this experiment, the students responded faster to concrete than to abstract sentences. This tends to show that people can comprehend concrete sentences—those they can create images for—more easily than they can comprehend abstract sentences.[15]

I think most of us would agree that these results are in accord with our intuitions. We would expect that concrete words (and concrete sentences made up of these words) would be easier for us to handle mentally than abstract words.

We can apply this information to our writing. We can rarely make nice substitutions of concrete words for abstract ones. However, there is a tendency for people writing gobbledygook to reach for the abstraction whenever possible (probably for the same reason they systematically prefer low-frequency words). How many times, for instance, have you seen cars called "vehicles" when the writer doesn't need the more abstract term? Airlines these days like to call their aircraft "equipment": "Flight 685 will be delayed due to lateness of the inbound equipment."

My favorite comes from an article on how to grade papers. Probably wanting to sound very impressive, the author uses the term "dichotomous scale"—apparently some sort of glorious device teachers can use.[16] It ends up that this "dichotomous scale" is simply a checklist: "Is the support in the student's paper good? Yes/No." "Is the student's paper well organized? Yes/No." A dichotomy is a division into two parts, so the dichotomy in this instance is "yes" or "no." I guess the author felt that "Yes/No Checklists" might not be of much interest, but people would be impressed with his discussion of "dichotomous scales."

The point is that unless you want to puff up what you're writing about at the expense of your reader's capability, you should use concrete words when you have a choice.

JARGON

The last item I'll cover in this chapter is jargon. Some people think of jargon as a synonym for all those words used by people who write some form of "-ese": bureaucratese, legalese, academese, and so forth. I use a more technical definition. I define jargon as the special vocabulary of a particular group. Lawyers have their words, doctors theirs, physicists theirs, and so forth. Jargon is not always something bad to use, either.

One jargon term I've been using is the word "process." In psycholinguistics, it means the intellectual operations of the brain. It's shorthand, and it makes a desirable analogy between the brain and the computer. You can probably think of jargon in your field. The Air Force, for example, uses "SAC" to stand for "Strategic Air Command," the organization that controls bombers and most intercontinental missiles (or "ICBM's"—another jargon term).[17]

When is jargon good and when is it bad? If people do not know your term, then it's bad. Don't use it.

On the other hand, if your readers do know the term, are very familiar with it, then you would probably be making a mistake to avoid it. For one thing, there is a certain undeniable psychological benefit to using a term that is "in." That way, you are "in," too. Also, using jargon at the right time may actually help your reader.

To explain, I'll need to use a couple of terms from the chapter on how we read. "Chunking," you will recall, means combining letters or words or ideas so that they become a single meaningful unit, thus taking up only one of the five or so slots in your short-term memory. "Automaticity" means that as people become more familiar with words, they can process them more automatically during the reading process. When they see an unfamiliar word, for example, readers must shift their attention to discovering its meaning—to looking it up in their mental dictionary. Since the brain is a limited capacity processor, a shift to the mental dictionary means less capability for the brain to make sense of the reading material.

People familiar with certain jargon terms, such as SAC, probably process them automatically, with no shift away from the long-term memory. So there should be no loss of efficiency in the reading process when people encounter familiar jargon.

Also, a jargon term for someone familiar with it probably stands as a single meaningful unit in the short-term memory, a single "chunk." On the other hand, longer versions, such as "Strategic Air Command" or, more especially, "the Air Force organization that controls most of our bombers and missiles," probably take up more slots in the short-term memory, filling several of the five or so slots. Thus, using jargon for the right audience makes sense from the standpoint of contemporary reading theory. Readers familiar with the jargon can process it automatically and, in terms of the short-term memory, efficiently.

Still, I think that there is seldom any problem from *underusing* jargon. The real problem comes from *overusing* it, from using terms that the reader is either unfamiliar with or only partially familiar with.[18] An intelligent writer will not assume that his reader knows everything that the writer does. After all, a reader who understands the jargon will still be able to understand what he's reading if the jargon is replaced with something explanatory. But a reader who does not understand the jargon will be lost if that is what he must read.

Now Richard Lanham, who wrote *Style: An Anti-Textbook*, says, ironically, "No one can deny that America in our time has produced the finest flowering of specialist gobbledygook the planet has seen."[18] He adds that the reason people write in jargon —and in gobbledygook —is not so much that they are careless of their readers or ignorant of how to write; instead, according to Lanham, they unconsciously wish to assert that they are part of a special group, a special world that shares a mysterious and beautifully erudite insight:

> What arcana they share! What bright chaps they must be to share them![19]

The rationale for writing indecipherably, then, according to Lanham, is the mutual "flattery, the ritual mystification that keeps the outsiders out and the insiders so pleased with themselves."[20]

It would be nice to believe Lanham, because he makes such perfectly good fun of the bureaucrats, academics, and other puffed up pontificators who sometimes intimidate us with their difficult writing. And I think that there is a certain amount of merit in what Lanham says. Yet he overstates.

Too many people make a sincere effort to communicate their ideas clearly, but are trapped—by habit, by a poor model of writing to follow, by their own uneasiness with the written word. Therefore, they try to imitate the "code" (the gobbledygook they see all around them), constantly translating their ideas into it.

I do not deny that there are some people with the unconscious motivation that Lanham articulates, yet I believe that most
people who write gobbledygook are little different from you and
me. They would like to communicate clearly if they knew how and
if they were convinced that such a style would be all right—
acceptable as "good" writing. That is why I try, in this book, to
show that the entrenched code of gobbledygook simply does not
communicate for physiological and psychological reasons, and
that a code that does communicate (an informal style) is perfectly
acceptable.

Notes for Chapter 6

1.   There are several sources showing that words can be easier to read because they have fewer syllables, because we acquired the words while we were
young, and because we have recently encountered them.

Marcel Adam Just and Patricia A. Carpenter, "A Theory of Reading: From
Eye Fixations to Comprehension," *Psychological Review,* 87, No. 4 (July 1980),
329-54, used a television camera to record the eye fixations of students reading
narrative material. Just and Carpenter found that "encoding time increased by 52
msec for each syllable" (p. 338). They also found that the students had shorter eye
fixations for second and later times they encountered a relatively low-frequency
word (pp. 339-40). They explain that once a word has been encountered, it is acti-
vated past a threshold of recognition. But it is only slowly that the word decays
back to its initial state. Thus, when a reader encounters it again shortly, the word
reaches the recognition threshold more quickly. Scarborough, Cortese, and Scarborough (cited in full below) had essentially the same finding in a different experiment. In fact, they found the effect could last as long as two days, but I am sure
that effect must have been for unusual words, though they do not say so.

My source for the theory that the age of acquisition is a factor in word
recognition is the following: John B. Carroll and Margaret N. White, "Age-of-
Acquisition Norms for 220 Picturable Nouns," *Journal of Verbal Learning and Verbal Behavior,* 12 (1973), 563-76. To obtain their data, the researchers asked college
students to guess when they had first learned words.

2.   Henry Kucera and W. Nelson Francis, *Computational Analysis of
Present-Day American English* (Providence, R.I.: Brown University Press, 1967). Interestingly, the first 135 words on the list account for 50% of the words we encounter per million (or whatever) words of text.

This analysis is not without its flaws, as the authors freely admit. Because
they used a computer, there is no distinction made between the meanings of
words. The frequency of "can" is for all of its meanings, as a verb and as a noun.

Also, variant spellings ("catalog" / "catalogue" and "non-conformist" / "nonconformist") are listed as separate words (xxi). Also, Foss and Hakes, cited in Chapter 4, point out that there can be families of words:

> For example, consider two words like "telegraphy" and "temerity." Both of these are rare words in English; each occurred only once in a sample of over one million words of naturally occurring text (Kucera & Francis, 1967). The words differ greatly in how familiar they seem, however. "Telegraphy" seems to be a much more familiar word. This might simply be due to a sampling error in the word count, but there is another, more plausible reason for this difference. "Telegraphy" has many related words (e.g., "telegraph," "telegrapher," etc.), while "temerity" has none. The sum of the frequencies of the items related to "telegraphy" is 38, a very large difference from a frequency of one. (pp. 107-8)

3. Don L. Scarborough, Charles Cortese, and Hollis S. Scarborough, "Frequency and Repetition Effects in Lexical Memory," *Journal of Experimental Psychology: Human Perception and Performance,* 3, No. 1 (February 1977), 1-17. These researchers were most interested in the effects of recently encountered words, but they confirmed the frequency effects also.

4. Just and Carpenter, p. 339.

5. Douglas Vipond, "Micro- and Macroprocesses in Text Comprehension," *Journal of Verbal Learning and Verbal Behavior,* 19 (1980), 291.

6. Vipond, p. 294.

7. Adapted from a handout, Executive Writing Course of the United States Air Force Academy.

8. Herta A. Murphy and Charles E. Peck, *Effective Business Communications,* 3d ed. (New York: McGraw-Hill, 1980), p. 78.

9. Handout, Executive Writing Course of the United States Air Force Academy.

10. Professor Paul Diehl pointed out to me that "utilize" once had a definition distinct from "use." It once meant, according to the Oxford English Dictionary, "To make oneself of use": "You come out here and utilize a little."

11. E.B. White, Introduction to *The Elements of Style,* 3d ed., by William Strunk and E.B. White (New York: Macmillan, 1979), p. xiii.

There's an interesting example on the denotative distinctions among words by Charles Fillmore as quoted by Richard C. Anderson and Peter Freebody, "Vocabulary Knowledge," in *Comprehension and Teaching,* ed. John T. Guthrie (Newark, Delaware: International Reading Association, 1981), p. 88:

> Consider an example involving verbs of visual perception. The basic verb is "see." If you notice that "look" involves a deliberate act of seeing, it can then be appreciated that "glimpse" refers to a short act of seeing whereas "glance" refers to a short act of looking. "Stare," on the other hand, refers to a prolonged act of looking. The variations in sense among these verbs can be understood in terms of just two semantic features, intention and duration. Further distinctions would

be required to encompass other verbs of visual perception such as "notice" and "examine."

12.   Edgar Dale and Jeanne S. Chall, *A Formula for Predicting Readability* (Columbus, Ohio: Ohio State University, n.d.).

13.   Allan Paivio, John C. Yuille, and Stephen A. Madigan, "Concreteness, Imagery, and Meaningfulness Values for 925 Nouns," *Journal of Experimental Psychology Monograph Supplement*, 76, No. 1, Part 2 (January 1968), 1-25. This article establishes values for just what the title says. For concreteness, with 7 as the maximum, "arrow" rates a 7.00, "elephant" a 7.00, "delirium" a 2.79, and "necessity" a 1.97. The numbers came from subjective ratings by college students.

14.   Allan Paivio and Kalman Csapo, "Picture Superiority in Free Recall: Imagery or Dual Coding?" *Cognitive Psychology*, 5 (1973), 182-86. Also, there's a good summary of some later experiments in Allan Paivio and Ian Begg's *Psychology of Language* (Englewood Cliffs, N.J.: Prentice-Hall, 1981), p. 192.

15.   Susan M. Belmore, et al., "Drawing Inferences from Concrete and Abstract Sentences," *Journal of Verbal Learning and Verbal Behavior*, 21 (1982), 338-51. The experiment shows faster reactions for concrete sentences not just when the second ("test") sentence was identical, but also when it was a paraphrase or when it required an inference: "The relative magnitude of the superiority of concrete sentences was 485 milliseconds for Paraphrases and 517 milliseconds for Inferences" (p. 346)—large and significant differences.

Belmore also had another variation. Half of the students would see an experimental sentence and then immediately see the test sentence. The other half of the students saw all of the experimental sentences first, waited 25 minutes and worked on some other material, and then responded to the test sentences. Again, the results in both cases consistently and significantly favored the concrete sentences.

16.   Charles R. Cooper, "Holistic Evaluation of Writing," in *Evaluating Writing*, ed. Charles R. Cooper and Lee Odell (n.p.: NCTE, 1977), pp. 8-9.

17.   For a clever article on jargon in the Pentagon, I recommend John G. Kester's "How to Speak Pentagonese: Translations from the Five-Sided World of the Military," *The Washingtonian*, February 1982, pp. 69-75. Kester was the Special Assistant to the Secretary of Defense, the single point of contact between the Department of Defense and the White House. Here are some examples of jargon from his article:

Ground zero: The hamburger stand in the middle of the Pentagon's center courtyard. [from the suspicion that the Pentagon might be a likely target for a nuclear attack]

Unkunks: Unknown unknowns. Things we not only don't know about, but don't even know we don't know about.

18.   Richard Lanham, *Style: An Anti-Textbook* (New Haven: Yale University Press, 1974), p. 68.

19.   Lanham, p. 72.

20.   Lanham, p. 72.

7   USE A NATURAL WORD ORDER

In the last chapter, we discussed the advantages to the writer and the reader of using simple words, words you might use in a friendly conversation. This chapter is about sentences.[1] Again, my advice is to use sentences that sound natural to you, sentences you could speak easily.[2] As with words, there are advantages both for the writer and for the reader.

There are three areas I'll cover in this chapter: first person, active and passive voice, and prepositions. I think writers often have trouble writing naturally in each of these areas.

Many writers of gobbledygook, for example, will do phenomenal gymnastic tricks with their word order just to avoid using the first person. Instead of saying, "We have decided that . . .," they'll say something like "It has been determined by members of the committee that. . . ." Instead of using a natural, spoken word order, in other words, they'll often distort that word order simply to follow what they mistakenly think is a convention of "good" writing.

One of the favorite ways gobbledygook writers have for avoiding first person is to use the passive voice, which is the second part of this chapter. In fact, the sample I just showed you, "It *has been determined* by members of the committee that . . ." is in the passive voice. Much more on this later, for the topic of passive voice is a much misunderstood one in the area of clear writing. And don't worry if you don't know what "passive voice" means. I'll define it for you.

In the last part of this chapter, I'll cover a lesser but very much related point: distorting the natural, spoken word order of sentences in order to avoid putting prepositions at the end of sentences. That's where such awkward sentences as the following come from: "That is a matter *with* which the committee has concerned itself" (instead of "That is a matter the committee has concerned itself *with*").

I'll begin by discussing the first person.

FIRST PERSON

The first person consists of the pronouns "I," "we," "me," "my," and so forth—words that refer to the writer either as an individual ("I") or as part of a group ("we").

Bureaucratic and other writers often go to great lengths to avoid referring to themselves in their writing. There are, I admit, times when the pronoun "I" is simply inappropriate.

For example, if you work for the State Department as a middle-level manager and write a report to the White House, a passage like this one wouldn't be appropriate:

> I found out from recent intelligence reports that Country X
> will have another bad wheat crop. Therefore, Janet Miller and I
> met with representatives from the Department of Agriculture.

Let's face it. If you're a middle-level manager, nobody in the White House is especially interested in what *you* think—at least as an individual. But they may care greatly what your *organization* thinks. When you're speaking for an organization, then, the word "I" is usually inappropriate unless you're the organization's head.

If there are times that you shouldn't use I, as in the statement above, then what should you do? Unfortunately, most people would choose this solution:

> A review of recent intelligence reports has been made, and it
> has been determined that Country X will have another bad

wheat crop. Representatives from our agency and representatives from the Department of Agriculture have met.

See what happens? The early stages of gobbledygook.

Now I intentionally didn't convert the passage into mature gobbledygook, instead making only the necessary changes to avoid first person. Mature gobbledygook would more likely resemble the following:

> Pursuant to White House directive, a thorough examination of pertinent recent intelligence materials has been conducted by this agency, and it has been determined that Country X will experience inferior agricultural harvests vis-a-vis their projected wheat crop. Subsequent to above-mentioned review, representatives of this agency contacted appropriate representatives in the Department of Agriculture in order to arrange for interagency coordination. Representatives of the agencies subsequently arranged for a meeting, which occurred one day prior to this date.

Fortunately, there's more than one way to get around the word "I." The answer is the word "we." "We" has the immense advantage of standing for individuals as individuals or as members of an organization. "We" can mean "Janet Miller and I" or it can mean "members of the State Department."

There would be nothing inappropriate at all, then, for the White House to receive this version of the passage:

> We found out from recent intelligence reports that Country X will have another bad wheat crop. Therefore, we met with representatives from the Department of Agriculture.

What about using first person in scientific and technical writing? There's a notion that scientific and technical writers must, above all, avoid first person, as though they are dealing so objectively with their material that it was never subjected to human frailty. If people aren't mentioned in a report, then there must not have been any people there to make mistakes. That, of course, is nonsense, as John Trimble points out nicely in *Writing with Style:*

> Since what we write is presumably what we believe and feel, it is logically inconsistent to put up the pretense that it is scientifically detached and Pure Thought, and that our words just

dropped out of thin air onto paper. Moreover, the pretense itself is a piece of absurdity. It's akin to ducking behind a screen
every time you say something in conversation so as to persuade your listener that he is hearing merely some Voice,
some disembodied intelligence, speaking to him.[3]

I think some of the best scientific writers have known this for
years. Remember in Chapter 4 I discussed the concept of "chunking"? George Miller originated the term in a famous article he published in 1956, "The Magical Number Seven, Plus or Minus Two."
Here's the introductory paragraph of that article. Notice that Miller
doesn't try to conceal his personality as he writes. Notice also his
use of first person:

> My problem is that I have been persecuted by an integer.
> For seven years this number has followed me around, has in-
> truded in my most private data, and has assaulted me from
> the pages of our most public journals. This number assumes a
> variety of disguises, being sometimes a little larger and some-
> times a little smaller than usual, but never changing so much
> as to be unrecognizable. The persistence with which this
> number plagues me is far more than a random accident.
> There is, to quote a famous senator, a design behind it, some
> pattern governing its appearances. Either there really is some-
> thing unusual about the number or else I am suffering from
> delusions of persecution.
>
>   I shall begin my case history by telling you about some ex-
> periments. . . .[4]

The personal style makes you want to keep reading, doesn't it? The
friendly, personable style is one advantage of the first person, yet
there are two other important advantages: first person is easier on
the reader, and it's easier on the writer.

Advantages of First Person for the Reader

In the last chapter we discussed some characteristics that make
words easier to read, including word frequency and concreteness.
First person words obviously have a high word frequency; in fact,
"I" ranks 20th in the language, and "we" ranks 41st—high, indeed.[5] First person words are also concrete. If they refer to specific
people, then they're very concrete. Even if they refer to unknown

people who work at the State Department, they are still relatively concrete. You wouldn't have mental images of specific people, but you would know the word referred to human beings with certain general characteristics.

Two reasons to favor first person words, then, are that they are common and relatively concrete: easy for the reader to "process." However, there's a more important reason. When a person writes in the first person, he naturally uses many first person words as subjects: "I noticed that . . ." and "We have since discovered that. . . ." There is a special advantage to readers when these words are subjects. Let me explain, for the point is important.

In Chapter 4 I said that the short-term memory can hold only five or so units of meaning and can hold them for only a short time. At the appropriate time—as soon as possible, but often at the ends of clauses or sentences—the information in the short-term memory integrates with the long-term memory, the place the brain makes sense of the reading material.

There's an advantage to the short-term memory if the subject and the verb are close together and if they come early in a sentence. Subjects usually don't make much sense by themselves, but a subject and a verb together often do—perhaps enough sense to begin integration with the long-term memory. For example, the subject "We" doesn't mean much by itself, but it does when combined with a verb: "We found out. . . ." Certainly a subject and a verb give the reader a good perspective on the rest of the sentence. If that perspective comes at the beginning of the sentence, then the reader is in good shape to understand what follows.

Here, for example, is a long sentence. In spite of its length, though, it's easy to read since the subject and the verb come early. The early subject and verb give a perspective for understanding the rest of the sentence.

> We found out that pirates have ships, that ants have hills, that teachers have blackboards, that computers have memories, that trees have limbs, that houses have rooms, that birds have wings, that grasshoppers have legs, that mountains have peaks, and that rivers have water.

See the advantage of having the subject and the verb come early? As you read each phrase after the subject and verb, you achieve some degree of "closure," almost certainly enough to integrate the material into the long-term memory. You don't have to hold the entire sentence in your short-term memory until you finish. That would be difficult or impossible, anyway.

Now let's consider the advantage of using first person words as subjects of sentences. First person words have an advantage that at first seems like a disadvantage: unlike the nouns they replace, they're hard to modify. When they begin a sentence, then, the verb almost has to follow them, thus giving the reader a good perspective on the rest of the sentence.

When a noun is the subject, on the other hand, it can have many modifiers before it and many between it and the verb—so many that the reader's short-term memory can overload or even erase.

Let's look at a couple of examples:

We found out from recent intelligence reports that. . . .

The annual regulatory monitorship review of intelligence reports from various federal agencies with agricultural overview responsibilities has been made. . . .

You can see what happens: the noun "review," as the subject, collects all sorts of words before and after it.[6] In fact, collecting modifiers is a common characteristic of gobbledygook. But the simple device of using first person, particularly as the subject of a sentence, almost forces the writer to put a subject and a verb right next to each other. That's an important advantage for the reader.

There may be another advantage to the reader that is less objective: I think readers are probably more interested in written material that refers to people (writing that has names and pronouns like "I," "you," "she" in it) than in written material that doesn't. Rudolf Flesch, who developed a well-known readability formula (for measuring how easy or difficult reading material is) has one version of his formula that measures "human interest."[7] In this version, you count the number of personal references in a passage. Then you can determine the reading ease: 19 or more personal references per hundred words in the passage equates to "very easy" reading; 6 personal references or more, "standard"; and 2 or fewer, "very difficult."[8]

I've never been comfortable with this sort of precision in measuring readability, but I do think that Flesch may be right that human interest is an important factor in how easy material is to read. In part, that ease is related to the objective matters I have just discussed—an early closure for the subject and verb, etc. But I think that there is also some value to the idea that we are simply interested in reading about people and their involvement with whatever our subject is.

Advantages of First Person for the Writer

There is another advantage of using the first person. It also can make the writing easier to write.

In Chapter 5, I emphasized the importance of writing the way you talk. That way, the words and ideas are not only expressed more clearly, but they also come more easily. However, if you don't use words like "I" and "we" when you write, you're going to have trouble writing the way you talk, aren't you? And if you have trouble writing the way you talk, you'll be back where you started.

Of course, some people have learned to talk in the third person: "It has been determined . . .," "The committee has decided . . .," etc. Still, I feel sure that those people also have a "voice" or role for speaking in the first person, too, especially in relaxed, informal situations. And I also feel sure that the informal voice is the more fluent of the two, simply because it functions in a relaxed, informal environment—an environment without additional pressure or constraints that can hamper their thinking and speaking (and, of course, their *writing*).

PASSIVE VOICE

This section on passive voice is closely related to the last one on the first person. The reason is that people who avoid using the first person almost force themselves to write in the passive voice.

Passive voice isn't always bad; in fact, there are definite circumstances when it is preferable to the active voice. Still, the passive voice, when misused (as it usually is), is one of the primary causes of unclear writing. It can place almost unbearable demands on the reader. (And on the unsure writer.)

Let's begin by defining it.

Definitions: Active and Passive Voice

Verbs are in either the active or the passive voice, but don't confuse a verb's *voice* with its *tense* (some common verb tenses are past, present, and future).[9] "Tense" describes one characteristic of a verb; "voice" (active or passive) describes another.

First, let's look at an illustration of sentences in active and passive voice. Then I'll explain them.

Active Voice: Phil ripped the paper bag.

Passive Voice: The paper bag was ripped by Phil.

Simply, in *active* voice, the *subject does whatever the verb says.* In the first example above, the subject is "Phil" and the verb is "ripped." The subject, in active voice, does the action: Phil rips.

In *passive* voice, the *subject has whatever the verb says done to it.* In the second example, the subject is "paper bag" and the verb is "was ripped." The subject is acted upon, then: The paper bag was ripped. The paper bag hasn't done anything; something has been done to it.

There are other, more objective ways to identify verbs in the passive voice:

1. Passive verbs always have a form of the verb "to be" as a helping verb:[10]

    The paper bag *was* ripped.
    The car has *been* hit.
    The tree will *be* struck by lightning.
    The groom *is* congratulated by the preacher.

2. Passive verbs always have a main verb that ends in "-ed" if it's a regular verb, or the equivalent, if it's an irregular verb:

    The paper bag was ripped. (regular verb)
    The car has been *hit*. (irregular verb)
    The tree will be *struck* by lightning. (irregular verb)
    The groom is congratulated by the preacher. (regular verb)

3. Sentences with passive verbs either have—or you could mentally add—a prepositional phrase that begins with "by":

> The paper bag was ripped (by Phil). (added)
> The car has been hit (by someone). (added)
> The tree will be struck *by lightning.*
> The groom is congratulated *by the preacher.*

If these three tests—and *all* of them have to apply for a verb to be passive—seem too technical, just fall back on the simpler one I gave: in the active voice, the subject does the acting; in the passive voice, something else does the acting.

In the four sample sentences above, then, we can tell the verbs are passive because the subjects aren't acting: the paper bag isn't doing the ripping, the car isn't doing the hitting, the tree isn't doing the striking, and the groom isn't doing the congratulating.

Some Reasons People Use the Passive Voice

Although most people use passive voice too often, there are times that it has its advantages.

You can use the passive voice to avoid mentioning yourself or whoever else performed the action of the verb. Let's say, for example, that your office has just made a controversial decision. In the letter that promulgates that decision, would you want to write this sentence?

I decided to close all the airports in the country.

That word "I" makes you seem awfully responsible, doesn't it? Suddenly, you're a target; you, the individual.

You can try to get around this by using the word "we," thus making your office, instead of you, seem responsible:

We decided to close all the airports in the country.

However, you may not particularly want your office to be a target, either. Let's try passive voice. First, we'll use passive with the "by" prepositional phrase:

It has been decided by us to close all airports in the country.

That helps, doesn't it? Now, with a verbal disappearing act, we can get both you and your office entirely out of the picture. We'll just eliminate that "by" prepositional phrase:

It has been decided to close all airports in the country.

Passive voice, then, is a great way to keep you or someone else from seeming responsible for anything. Many people outside the bureaucracy think that bureaucrats use it intentionally to shirk responsibility. I'm sure that's true to a certain extent. However, from my three years working in the bureaucracy, I think there are several other reasons people in the bureaucracy—and elsewhere—use it.

First, sometimes the actor, the person or the office responsible, simply isn't important. If, for instance, you want to tell people in your organization that a new regulation has been approved, the person or office who approved it is probably irrelevant:

Carl Ronson has approved the new regulation.

Passive voice then eliminates the irrelevant person:

The new regulation has been approved.

A second reason people use the passive voice is to put the emphasis on the right word in the sentence.[11] If, for example, you're talking about a regulation in one sentence, you might want to make it the subject of the next, thus providing good coherence:

We finally have good news on the new regulation. The new regulation has been approved.

A third reason people use the passive voice isn't so good, yet it's probably the main one: they simply are avoiding using first person. I remember hearing in school that I shouldn't use the word "I" because that would mean I was an egotist. Somehow that logic doesn't make much sense, does it? Yet people who have grown up in other ways still carry that thought around with them because some teacher in some school once said it.

The fourth reason people use the passive is closely related to the third one: inertia. They know a few catch phrases, such as "It *has been determined* . . ." or "This review *is based upon*. . . ." They start with passive voice and just stay there, writing one passive after another, unable or unwilling to leave the mental track they're on.

Yet there are good reasons to leave that track.

The Disadvantages of Passive Voice

Actually, there's no strong view in reading theory that readers have any more difficulty reading either active or passive voice. For example, you should be able to read either of these two sentences with about the same degree of ease:

Active Voice: Phil ripped the paper bag.

Passive Voice: The paper bag was ripped.

Now early research tended to show that passives took longer for people to read.[12] In one experiment, people would see either a sentence or a picture and be asked if the two communicated the same act. For example, people would see a picture of a car and a truck colliding. They'd also see one of two sentences:

The car hit the truck. (Active Voice)

The truck was hit by the car. (Passive Voice)

The people took longer to respond to the *passive* sentence and the picture than to the *active* sentence and the picture.

Later research, however, maintains that the brain processes sentences and pictures differently, so the earlier experiments are not valid. The opinion today is that active and passive sentences take about the same time to read, but *either* can take longer or shorter, depending on the context.

So what is the problem with passive voice? The problem is not the passive voice itself but what it does to the rest of the sentence. And what it does can cause great difficulty for the reader.

As I said earlier, the primary reason people write passive voice is to avoid using first person words. To get themselves out of the picture, they simply shift themselves to that "by" prepositional phrase and then delete it:

> We found out from recent intelligence reports . . .
>
> BECOMES
>
> A review of recent intelligence reports *has been made* (by us) . . .

Passive voice, then, often causes the same problems that avoiding the first person does. It moves the words "I" and "we" out of the subject position, too often replacing them with abstract, low-frequency nouns. Then those nouns can build up modifiers that strain the reader's short-term memory.

Passive voice is also hard on the writer, and for the same reason that avoiding first person words was hard on him. Many people write passive voice to avoid using first person words. Therefore, they have trouble writing the way they talk. After all, few people talk without using "I's" and "we's."

Again, if you try to use a natural word order for your sentences, the kind you might use in a friendly conversation, you won't find yourself lapsing into habitual passive voice. If you imagine yourself talking to your reader, you'll almost certainly use mainly first person words and active voice. When you do use passive voice, it will then be for one of the good reasons: leaving out irrelevant people or things, or keeping the emphasis where it belongs.

There's nothing wrong with using the passive voice at the right time; there are many, many right times that exist, especially to get the emphasis right. But too many writers use passive voice almost all of the time. And, as we have seen, the damage can be considerable.

PREPOSITIONS

Would you be uneasy if you had to end a sentence with a preposition? Most people do it all the time in speech: "That's something we'll have to talk *about.*" In writing, though, these same people often do verbal gymnastics to shift that preposition somewhere toward the middle: "That's something *about* which we'll have to talk."

I admit that if you decide to put prepositions at the end, you won't make a giant step toward readability: after all, there simply aren't many opportunities to end sentences with prepositions, anyway. But you will gain one more technique—if only a small one—to make your writing more like your talking. Besides, there's more than ample authority to put prepositions at the ends of sentences.

For example, even a source that tries to serve as an authority for putting prepositions in the middle unwittingly violates its own rule. Here's an excerpt from the first popular English grammar, published by Bishop Lowth in 1762. Notice what happens to the Bishop in the sentence that begins "This is":

> The preposition is often separated from the relative which it governs, and joined to the verb at the end of the sentence, or of some member of it: as, "Horace is an author, *whom* I am much delighted *with.*" "The world is too well-bred, to shock authors with a truth, *which* generally their booksellers are the first to inform them *of.*" This is an idiom, which our language is strongly inclined to: it prevails in common conversation, and suits very well with the familiar style in writing: but the placing of the preposition before the relative, is more graceful, as well as more perspicuous; and agrees much better with the solemn and elevated style.[13]

Bishop Lowth violates his own rule at the very moment he preaches it: "This is an idiom, *which* our language is strongly inclined *to* . . ." [Emphasis mine][14]. Another interesting point is that the second of Lowth's examples showing "poor" use of a preposition is by the great poet Alexander Pope, considerably more noted for his writing than the author of the grammar book.

Recent grammarians are apt to be more lenient than Lowth, perhaps not so committed to a "solemn and elevated style." H. W. Fowler, in *A Dictionary of Modern Usage*, includes a well-known essay strongly supporting the use of prepositions at the ends of sentences. Fowler's book, first published in 1926 and rather conservative, is one of the most famous ever written on the English language.

It is a cherished superstition that prepositions must, in spite of the incurable English instinct for putting them late . . . be kept true to their name & placed before the word they govern. "A sentence ending in a preposition is an inelegant sentence" represents a very general belief. . . .

Those who lay down the universal principle that final prepositions are "inelegant" are unconsciously trying to deprive the English language of a valuable idiomatic resource, which has been used freely by all our greatest writers except those whose instinct for English idiom has been overpowered by notions of correctness derived from Latin standards. The legitimacy of the prepositional ending in literary English must be uncompromisingly maintained. . . .

If it were not presumptuous . . . to offer advice, the advice would be: Follow no arbitrary rule, but remember that there are often two or more possible arrangements between which a choice should be consciously made; if the abnormal, or at least unorthodox, final preposition that has naturally presented itself sounds comfortable, keep it; if it does not sound comfortable, still keep it if it has compensating vigour, or when among awkward possibilities it is the least awkward.[15]

Fowler gives good advice. There's no reason to write tangled sentences simply to follow some rule that many good writers ignore, anyway.

If you don't accept Fowler's rationale, perhaps Winston Churchill can persuade you. When someone corrected him for ending a sentence with a preposition, he made this perfect rejoinder: "This is the type of arrant pedantry, up with which I shall not put."[16]

Notes for Chapter 7

1. I'll discuss sentences further in Chapter 10.

2. Of course, some people have odd natural speech. Thus, to tell them to use a natural word order may not be very helpful. Still, as I point out later in this chapter, I believe that virtually all people have what we might consider a "natural" voice that they use sometime, somewhere, especially when they are relaxed with intimate friends in an informal setting.

3. John Trimble, *Writing with Style* (Englewood Cliffs, N.J.: Prentice-Hall,

1975), p. 90. Trimble lists what he calls the "Seven Nevers," the "Core Rules" of the TOTELarian ideology (TOTEL, you will recall, means "The One True English Language Sect"):

1. Never begin a sentence with "and" or "but."
2. Never use contractions.
3. Never refer to the reader as "you."
4. Never use the first-person pronoun, "I."
5. Never end a sentence with a preposition.
6. Never split an infinitive.
7. Never write a paragraph containing only a single sentence. (p. 85)

4. George A. Miller, "The Magical Number Seven, Plus or Minus Two: Some Limits on Our Capacity for Processing Information," *The Psychological Review*, 63, No. 2 (March 1956), 81.

5. Henry Kucera and W. Nelson Francis, *Computational Analysis of Present-Day American English* (Providence, R.I.: Brown University Press, 1967).

6. People could simply restrain themselves from writing strings of modifiers without resorting to using the first person and active voice. Yet since the first person, in itself, is a valuable asset for readability, such restraint would be admirable but misplaced.

7. Rudolf Flesch, *The Art of Plain Talk* (New York: Harpers, 1946), pp. 48-57. In a way, by introducing the relationship between the writer and the reader as a significant factor in clear writing, I am saying that more than just the form of the language is significant, that rhetorical concerns may be important, too. I think that would be hard to deny.

8. Flesch, p. 205.

9. Books on clear writing like to stay away from passive voice, despite its importance, since it's hard to define for laymen. Rudolf Flesch, in *On Business Communications* (cited in full at the end of Chapter 5), spends only one page of the book on passive voice. He starts out, perhaps wisely, "So, since I know from experience that a grammatical definition of the passive voice won't do much good, I'll illustrate" (p. 21). He then gives six examples, some including several sentences, apparently hoping people can learn that way.

Robert Gunning, in *The Technique of Clear Writing* (also cited in full in Chapter 5), mentions passives only on one page and only in passing.

10. I realize that I'm simplifying here by omitting the "get" passive: "The rabbit *GOT beaten* by the turtle."

11. A paper by Paul Diehl, Richard Lloyd-Jones, John Mellon, and Carl Klaus (Correlation of Syntactic / Stylistic Fluency and Judgment with Rhetorical Fluency and Judgment in the Persuasive Writing of 17-Year Olds) makes a good point about the advantage to coherence of letting the subject matter determine whether a sentence should be active or passive:

> The passive construction allows writers to continue focusing on a subject across clauses even as that subject shifts back and forth from being an agent to being an object of some other agent. This ability

and the willingness to use it is important in establishing arguments, clauses linked together by some thread of logic. . . .

12.   There's a good summary of the research in the following book: Sam Glucksberg and Joseph H. Danks, *Experimental Psycholinguistics: An Introduction* (New York: Lawrence Erlbaum Associates, 1975), pp. 96-100.

13.   Robert Lowth, *A Short Introduction to English Grammar* (Delmar, N.Y.: Scholars' Facsimiles & Reprints, 1979), pp. 95-96.

14.   Charlotte Downey points out this inconsistency in her introduction to Lowth's book, p. xiv.

15.   H. W. Fowler, *A Dictionary of Modern English Usage* (London: Oxford University Press, 1926), pp. 457-59. Both Trimble and Flesch quote from this essay, although they do not quote the same excerpts I do.

16.   Quoted by Rudolf Flesch, *The Art of Readable Writing* (New York: Collier Books, 1949), p. 149.

8　DON'T OVERDO CONCISENESS

In Chapter 6, I quoted E.B. White's famous description of Will Strunk crying out, "Rule Seventeen. Omit needless words! Omit needless words! Omit needless words!" Obviously White was having a bit of fun with Strunk who repeats himself not once but twice in the very act of urging conciseness. Somewhat reminiscent of Bishop Lowth and his concern with prepositions, isn't it? Unfortunately, Strunk's advice—his Rule Seventeen—is no better than the Bishop's.

I know it seems incredible that I would take issue with conciseness. After all, the most cherished cliche about writing is that it should be "clear and concise." Yet if conciseness means only omitting words, then I have to disagree.

For example, some texts on clear writing urge writers to delete all unnecessary "which's" and "that's." Here's what Rudolf Flesch says in *On Business Communications:*

> The English language, it so happens, has the immensely practical device of leaving out the word *that* whenever you can express the sense of your sentence without it. And since *that* is one of the most frequently used words in the language, there's an opportunity to do it in almost every paragraph you write.[1]

Flesch, then, is a "word counter": the fewer words, the better for the writer and the reader.

Let's follow his advice and see what happens. I've already taken the "that" out of this sentence:

> The college students finally discovered the errors, mostly ty-pographical, were impossible to find.

Did you think, at first, that the students had actually discovered the errors? Omitting the "that" makes you misread the sentence. Now let's put the "that" back in:

> The college students finally discovered *that* the errors, mostly typographical, were impossible to find.

The point of this example is not that you should keep all of your "that's." Sometimes you can be more conversational by elimi-nating them. The point is that *saving words doesn't necessarily save your readers time or energy*. In the special case above, omitting a "that" almost guarantees that readers will have to re-read the sentence, thus demanding more rather than less from them. That may be conciseness, but it isn't efficiency.

In this chapter, I'll cover four areas where writers, often in an effort to be concise, actually end up being more demanding of their readers: writing strings of modifiers, using abbreviations, omitting inferences, and failing to use examples.

DON'T USE STRINGS OF MODIFIERS

I remember an incident that happened to me in Washington when I was taking a short report to other offices for approval. One person took a pencil to my report, eliminating some of the words. He was, he advised me, "making the report more concise." Here's what he did:

> *Original Version:* "The committee responsible for examining the institution . . ."
>
> *His Version:* "The institution examination committee . . ."

"See!" he proudly said. "I've saved you *three* words!" He had, too: "responsible," "for," and "the." He had also made the passage almost unreadable.

In his zeal for conciseness, he had wreaked instant havoc on the reading process:

1.   He put the three most difficult words—"institution examination committee"—right next to each other. That means the mental dictionary has to work overtime for three words in a row. Since the material in the short-term memory erases quickly if it isn't used, the first word may erase while the readers look up the second. When they finally get those two words in their short-term memories, the words may erase while they look up the third.

2.   He took out important words that show the relationship between two of the difficult words: "responsible for." He also successfully hid the relationships among the words in another way: he converted the verbal "examining" into a noun, "examination"— and then used it as a modifier!

I'm afraid the kind of "editing" I have just showed you takes place all the time. People eliminate a few short words, but those words are often prepositions and articles that help separate big words and help show relationships between them. Such "economy" is decidedly false.

In fact, some of the most unreadable gobbledygook comes from just that kind of false economy—jamming big words together to eliminate a few small but important ones. Let me show you some more examples of real gobbledygook.

Remember in Chapter 1 I quoted an excerpt from some Congressional testimony by the Army? That testimony was loaded with strings of big words, many of them nouns, jammed together. Here are some of them:

projected aircraft inventory
allowable time-between-overhaul
airframe overhaul requirements
reliability centered maintenance strategies
missile overhaul requirements
missile system end items

Don't be penny wise and pound foolish. If you find yourself
automatically stringing together big words, unstring them. Do the
opposite of the fellow with the pencil. Trade conciseness for efficiency.

There's a clever and facetious device that Philip Broughton
created to make fun of those strings of unprocessible words. He
calls it the "Systematic Buzz Phrase Projector," and it's shown in
Figure 5.

Column 1	Column 2	Column 3
0. Integrated	0. Management	0. Options
1. Total	1. Organizational	1. Flexibility
2. Systematized	2. Monitored	2. Capability
3. Parallel	3. Reciprocal	3. Mobility
4. Functional	4. Digital	4. Programming
5. Responsive	5. Logistical	5. Concept
6. Optional	6. Transitional	6. Time-phase
7. Synchronized	7. Incremental	7. Projection
8. Compatible	8. Third-generation	8. Hardware
9. Balanced	9. Policy	9. Contingency

Figure 5.   Buzz Phrase Projector[2]

To use the Buzz Phrase Projector, just pick any three-digit number.
The Buzz Phrase Projector will then produce for you, automatically, an impressive, all-purpose phrase. The number 248, for example, translates to "systematized digital hardware." Unfortunately, it doesn't mean anything.

Try a number yourself.

"No one will have the remotest idea of what you're talking
about," says Broughton. "But the important thing is that they're
not about to admit it."[3]

DON'T OVERUSE ABBREVIATIONS AND
ACRONYMS

Some people believe they can be concise not just by omitting
words but by omitting letters, too. They think that since abbreviations and acronyms (words created from the initials of other

words) take up less space on the page, the reader must be doing less work. But, as we have seen, there are better measures of a reader's effort than the centimeters of black marks on a page.

You've probably read reports loaded with abbreviations. Often the writer defines them the first time, then having "done his duty," uses them freely after that. Here are two brief examples:

> Once you've opened an Individual Retirement Account (IRA), you will be saving for your future. In fact, the IRA....

> The key to survival is the World-Wide Military Command and Control System (WWMCCS). When the WWMCCS....

You're perhaps already familiar with the acronym "IRA." When you see it in an article, then, you probably don't have any trouble understanding it to mean "Individual Retirement Account." In fact, you may be more used to the acronym than to what it stands for. So when the writer uses only the acronym in the second sentence, after defining it in the first, you have no trouble reading it. But that's not because of his definition. That's because you already knew the term—you had long since gained some degree of "automaticity" for it.

You're probably not familiar with the second term, WWMCCS. If I asked you to define it right now (don't look back!), could you do it? Probably not. That's because you haven't gained automaticity for it. In my example above, you would probably understand the term in the second sentence, immediately after it was defined. However, you probably would have trouble a paragraph or a page later. And what would happen if the writer used not just one unfamiliar abbreviation but several of them? You'd slow down on each one. Or stop. Or, more likely after awhile, skim on by.

If you find yourself, as a writer, putting abbreviations or acronyms in parentheses after their longer versions, you should ask yourself why. If your readers already know the short version, then the term needs no definition. If they don't know the short version, then don't expect them to memorize it on the spot and use it with ease ever after. Memorizing and reading are quite different mental activities, and you can guess which one takes more time and mental effort.

To memorize something, we have to put it not in the short-term memory but in the long-term memory.

In *Understanding Reading*, Frank Smith makes a couple of nice points about memorization. Here's what he says about holding telephone numbers in the *short*-term memory:

> A sequence of seven unrelated digits is about as much as anyone can retain. It is as if a benevolent providence had provided humanity with just sufficient short-term memory capacity to make telephone calls and then had failed to prophesy area codes. For if we try to hold more than six or seven items in short-term memory, then something will be lost. If someone distracts us when we are on our way to make that telephone call, perhaps by asking us the time of day or the location of a room, then some or all of the telephone number will be forgotten and there will be absolutely no point in standing around cudgelling our brains for the number to come back. We shall just have to return and ascertain the number once again.[4]

That's what happens when we come across an abbreviation or a jargon term sometime after it was first defined for us. If we didn't memorize it the first time—which we usually don't do—then the information in between erases it from our short-term memory. Since we didn't memorize it, we didn't put it in our long-term memory.

What if we had memorized it? That, as Frank Smith says, takes much more effort:

> To put one item into long-term memory takes five seconds—and in that five seconds there is little attention left over for anything else at all. The telephone number which will tax short-term memory to its capacity is at least accepted as quickly as it is read or heard, but to hold the same number in long-term memory, so that it can be dialed the next day, will require a good half minute of concentration, five seconds for each digit.[5]

How, then, should you use abbreviations and acronyms? If you don't use a term more than a couple of times, or if the times you use it are spread out, then go ahead and use the full term. If you use a term very frequently, then you should "teach" it to your reader: use it in the long version and then define it, but not in parentheses:

> Once you've opened an Individual Retirement Account—
> called an "IRA" for short—you will be saving for your future.
> In fact, the IRA . . .

If you then don't use the term for awhile, you'll have to define it
again.

Another solution is to use a synonym or a short form of the
term (using the full term every time could be very tedious, especially if it's lengthy):

> Once you've opened an Individual Retirement Account, you
> will be saving for your future. This new retirement plan . . .

These are solutions that don't ask your reader to become a memory expert.

Acronyms can be useful, of course. Sometimes a pronounceable abbreviation like "IRA" can save a mouthful, literally for a
speaker and metaphorically for a writer. Still, the problem with
gobbledygook writers is not that they use too few abbreviations.
Rather, they use too many.

However, saving letters may be a form of conciseness, but like
converting phrases into strings of difficult words, it's not a form of
efficiency.

DON'T REQUIRE INFERENCES

I remember once working with a woman whose job was to answer
fairly technical questions to inquiries by the general public. Yet she
steadfastly wrote as though her readers knew everything she did.
When asked to revise her letters to make them more simple, or
when asked to provide more background to her technical answers,
she'd usually say something like the following: "If these people
aren't smart enough to figure *that* out. . . ." Of course, the matter
was simple to her because she had been working in her own narrow area for years. She just couldn't see the world through the eyes
of others.

A term from reading theory helps describe her problem:
"schemata." Remember in the four versions of the poem "Mary
had a little lamb," the readers had to know all about veterinarians,

nursery rhymes, ownership, pets, etc., to understand them? That meant people had acquired the necessary "schemata" in those areas.

The woman I was talking about had a number of schemata in her technical area, yet the people inquiring from the general public didn't have them. The woman simply couldn't understand, or adjust to, their "ignorance."

As a writer, you have the difficult task of deciding just what your readers do and do not know. If you assume that they do have certain schemata, or knowledge, and they don't, then you won't communicate. On the other hand, if you assume they don't have certain schemata and it turns out that they do, you risk boring them or, even worse, making them feel that you are being condescending toward them.

In these larger matters, I can only advise you to use your best judgment. However, in a related matter—the demands on your readers to make inferences—I can offer more help.

First, let me explain what an inference is. Basically, you make an inference if you derive something unstated by using your ability to reason. For example, if I tell you that a box is to the right of a tree, you can infer that the tree is to the left of the box.[6] That one is easy.

Here's another one, this one provided by David Pearson in an article he wrote.[7] If you see these two sentences next to each other, you can probably infer the cause and effect relationship between them:

The chain broke. The machine stopped.

You can infer, from those two sentences, something a little more complex: "because the chain broke, the machine stopped."

We're all familiar, at least to some extent, with chains and machines. We have enough of the necessary schemata to make the necessary inference if we have only the two simple sentences without the cause/effect word, "because." What would happen, though, if we didn't have the necessary schemata? As David Pearson asks, would children be able to make the necessary inference from these two sentences:

> The new king clamped down on public meetings. Many residents emigrated to a new land.

Young children don't have the necessary schemata on politics, freedom of speech, etc., to make the necessary inference that the king's act probably caused the emigration.[8]

What if your readers don't have the necessary schemata for your topic? Then you have to be especially careful not to ask them to infer too much. You must be careful, in other words, eliminating links in your chain of reasoning, even though to do so would save you and your reader some words.

Even if your readers have the essential schemata, you should be especially careful demanding inferences from them. Reading and simultaneously making inferences is not easy.

Let me summarize an interesting experiment on that point. Susan Haviland and Herbert Clark asked people to read pairs of sentences.[9] One pair required an inference:

> Last Christmas, Eugene went to a lot of parties. This Christmas he got very drunk again.

The inference is that Eugene must have gotten drunk at those parties last Christmas. The researchers also asked people to read similar sentences that didn't require an inference:

> Last Christmas Eugene became absolutely smashed. This Christmas he got very drunk again.

By a significant margin, readers took longer to read the first set of sentences—those requiring inferences—than the second set.

These results are important for us as writers: even when our readers do have the necessary schemata, even when the required inference is simple for them to make, we are placing an extra demand on their mental resources. We may occasionally save a few words by asking our readers to infer what we do not say. But even smart people, good readers with the right knowledge of the subject, take longer to read when they have to make inferences at the same time. Don't make your readers work any harder than they have to; reading is demanding enough.

DON'T OMIT THE EXAMPLES

One of the worst economies you can make is to save words by leaving out examples. If you really want to make a point—drive it home, make it stick—then you *must* give examples.

Why is that so? In the chapter on using simple words, I showed that we understand both concrete words and concrete sentences better than abstract words and abstract sentences. If we can visualize something—imagine it—we can comprehend it better. If, say, you're writing a letter about the damage automobile pollution causes to the environment, you won't make your point very forcefully if you stay at that abstract level.

But what if you give an example of what is happening in Denver, Colorado? You can cite the statistics for two decades ago and for now. You can tell your own story of driving into the city and seeing only brown haze instead of Long's Peak. By spending a paragraph or several pages on such illustrations, you're certainly using more words—you're not being "concise." Yet you are making one instance of pollution vivid for your reader. The images you create for him will stay with him much longer than an abstract sentence or paragraph on the ills of auto pollution.

Furthermore, examples are not only apt to be the most interesting part of your writing, but they're also likely to be easier to read. An experiment by Graesser, Hoffman, and Clark using various types of writing showed that people read narrative writing faster than any other kind.[10] Narrative writing means writing that tells a story—such as your drive into Denver. Since many examples, especially the memorable ones, tell stories that illustrate points, examples are often easier for the reader to comprehend.

The lesson of this chapter, then, is that you should not make conciseness—the saving of words—your single most important goal. Don't pad your writing, of course, and don't tell your readers how to build a watch if they just want to know the time.[11] But don't leave out the examples, don't force your reader to make unnecessary inferences, don't pepper your writing with abbreviations, and don't turn perfectly good phrases into densely packed strings of nouns and other modifiers. If that's conciseness, it's the wrong kind. And, as I've emphasized throughout, it certainly isn't efficiency.

Notes for Chapter 8

1. Rudolf Flesch, *On Business Communications* (New York: Barnes and Noble, 1972), p. 16.

I like many things about Flesch's book—especially his emphasis on informal writing—but his advice to eliminate "that" is not one of them. He also advises leaving out "which" wherever possible: "you should also go on a 'which' hunt" (p. 17).

Like Trimble in *Writing with Style*, Flesch has seven rules. (We can assume Trimble meant the reverse of what he said—since his rules were ascribed to the TOTELS.) These are Flesch's rules:

1. Use contractions like *it's* or *doesn't*.
2. Leave out *that* whenever possible.
3. Use direct questions.
4. Use the pronouns *I, we, you*, and *they* as much as possible. Avoid using *it* and the passive voice.
5. If possible, put prepositions at the end.
6. When you refer back to a noun, repeat the noun or use a pronoun. Don't use "elegant variation."
7. Don't refer to what you *wrote* or are going to *write*, but to what you *talked about* or are going to *talk about*. Don't use such words as *above, below,* or *hereafter*; instead, say *earlier, later, from now on*.

Naturally, I agree with much of what Flesch says.

2. Philip Broughton, "How to Win at Wordsmanship" (box insert), *Newsweek*, May 6, 1968, p. 104.

3. Broughton, p. 104.

4. Frank Smith, *Understanding Reading*, 2d ed. (New York: Holt, Rinehart and Winston, 1978), p. 47.

5. Smith, p. 50.

6. Bransford and Johnson (cited in full in Chapter 4) mention this example of the tree and the box. They're not defining "inference," though, but making an interesting point about the long-term memory. They showed experimental subjects this passage:

> There is a tree with a box beside it, and a chair is on top of the box. The box is to the right of the tree. The tree is green and extremely tall. (p. 386)

Afterwards, the subjects saw several sentences:

> In a recognition task in which subjects were asked to choose which sentence they had actually heard from a set of alternatives, subjects were much more likely to choose a sentence like *The tree is to the left of the chair* than they were to choose a sentence that violated the overall set of relationships, e.g., *The chair is to the left of the tree.* (p. 386)

7. P. David Pearson, "The Effects of Grammatical Complexity on Children's Comprehension, Recall, and Conception of Certain Semantic Relations," *Reading Research Quarterly*, 10, No. 2 (1974-75), 190.

8. Pearson, p. 190.

9. Susan E. Haviland and Herbert H. Clark, "What's New? Acquiring New Information as a Process in Comprehension," *Journal of Verbal Learning and Verbal Behavior*, 13 (1974), 517. This is an excellent article. Its purpose is to show that one way our brain processes information is probably to take what is given—what it already knows, sometimes from the immediate context—and then to store whatever is new in a sentence with it. This is called the "Given-New Strategy."

I am also indebted to Professor Richard Lloyd-Jones for noting that sometimes an inference can have a desirable effect: "a small inference may create dramatic power with a sudden resolution." Thus, the reader making the inference will more likely understand your point, internalize it, because his consciousness was drawn to it by the necessity of making the inference. I suggest, however, that this should be a tool the writer reserves for very special occasions.

10. Arthur C. Graesser, Nicholas L. Hoffman, and Leslie F. Clark, "Structural Components of Reading Time," *Journal of Verbal Learning and Verbal Behavior*, 19 (1980), 148:

> The most robust predictor of reading time throughout this study was the narrativity of the passage. Narrative passages (stories) are read faster than expository passages. A 12-word sentence in a prototypical expository passage takes 1686 more milliseconds to read than a comparable sentence in a prototypical narrative passage. (p. 148)

People specializing in writing know, however, the difficulty of designating passages as entirely expository or entirely narrative. The difficulty could be much greater dealing with only 12-word sentences. There may be reason, then, to be suspicious of the findings.

11. This is a common saying in the Pentagon.

9 GIVE THE READER "ROAD SIGNS"

For the past four chapters, I have been urging you to write the way you talk. This chapter tempers that advice slightly.

When you're talking with someone, you usually don't have the time or occasion to be sure that your sentences are gems of style, expressing precisely what you think and moving smoothly and logically from one idea to the next. Yet the very fact that you're talking to someone rather than writing to him enables you to correct for occasional incoherence. You can rephrase your idea if you get some feedback that he doesn't understand what you're saying; you can shrug or use facial gestures as you talk to add another dimension to your communication; or you can use a different tone of voice to show that you're moving on to another point, drawing a conclusion, and so forth.

This chapter, then, will not ask you to write the way you talk but rather to use the advantages of being a writer—that is, having the time to think ahead and to revise—to give *written* signals of the flow of your writing.

When you're writing and finish a sentence, there are usually many directions you could take for the next sentence. You could continue to explain the first sentence; you could draw a conclusion from it; you could add another point similar to it; you could contradict it; you could modify it slightly; or you could start a new subject.

Think, then, of the reader's position as he finishes one of your sentences: usually he's not entirely certain what will follow. Yet if you can give him a clue at the beginning of that next sentence—a "road sign" telling him which road he is about to travel—he will have a much greater chance of understanding that sentence easily.

More specifically, a writer needs to use transitional words (such as "however," "yet," and "because") and other such devices to keep readers from getting lost. That's what this chapter is about. First, though, let me describe a fascinating experiment that will help me explain the rationale for using transitional devices.

Bransford and Johnson constructed an experimental paragraph that most people have trouble understanding even though the words are easy. Here it is:

> The procedure is actually quite simple. First you arrange things into different groups. Of course, one pile may be sufficient depending on how much there is to do. If you have to go somewhere else due to lack of facilities that is the next step; otherwise you are pretty well set. It is important not to overdo things. That is, it is better to do too few things at once than too many. In the short run this may not seem important but complications can easily arise. A mistake can be expensive as well. At first the whole procedure will seem complicated. Soon, however, it will become just another facet of life. It is difficult to foresee any end to the necessity for this task in the immediate future, but then one can never tell. After the procedure is completed one arranges the materials into different groups again. Then they can be put into their appropriate places. Eventually they will be used once more and the whole cycle will then have to be repeated. However, that is part of life.[1]

It doesn't seem to make much sense, does it? Now reread it, and this time I'll tell you the subject: washing clothes. By the way, one person reading this passage, a Washington bureaucrat, said that it described his job as a paper pusher.[2]

For their experiment, Bransford and Johnson used three different groups of people. They gave the first group the topic ("wash ing clothes") beforehand and then had them read the paragraph. The second group read the paragraph without ever seeing the topic. The third group read the paragraph and then saw the topic; but unlike you, they didn't have the opportunity then to reread it.

Next, all three groups took tests on their recall and comprehension. As you would suspect, the group that had the topic in advance did very well. The group that didn't get the topic at all did poorly. But here is the interesting part: the group that got the topic *after* reading the passage also did poorly—even slightly worse than the group that never did get it.

The conclusion is quite important for us: readers need a perspective either before they read something or as they read it. If they don't get the right perspective until afterward, they cannot reconstruct. They will either have to reread or continue in ignorance.

Remember the woman I mentioned in the last chapter who simply couldn't put herself in the place of her readers? When supervisors had trouble understanding her writing, she would sometimes point to her letter and say, "Well, I explain that down here!" As the Bransford and Johnson experiment shows, explaining something "down here" isn't much help when the reader is still "up there."

The fact that you provide the perspective somewhere in your letter or report isn't good enough: you have to provide it early. Readers cannot reconstruct. They can only reread.

I think that applies at the sentence-to-sentence level, too. If you can give your readers the right perspective as they enter a sentence—if you can give them a "road sign" to show them where they're headed—then they will have the right perspective on that sentence and will be able to comprehend it better.

There are countless ways to move smoothly and logically from one sentence to the next. This area of investigation is, in fact, a very complex one. In fact, there are so many subtle methods we have in English to signal the relationships between ideas, that specialists in language and writing find the areas of cohesion and coherence enticing for further investigation. I will not go into some of the complexities involved.

Yet there are a few relatively simple and specific techniques that can help most writers write more clearly: (1) using more transitional words and phrases, and (2) using informal punctuation. These techniques are two good ways of signaling the relationship between two sentences, or parts of sentences.

USE TRANSITIONAL WORDS AND PHRASES

A major symptom of gobbledygook is that far too many sentences begin with the subject of an independent clause or its modifiers. In Chapter 1, I quoted four examples of gobbledygook, one each from the government, from the military, from business, and from academia. In those examples, you didn't see any sentences beginning like this: "On the other hand. . . ." Or like this: "Yet. . . ." Or like this: "Although. . . ."

Those are all transitional words and phrases—"road signs" that let the reader know where the next sentence is taking him.

In the gobbledygook I quoted in Chapter 1, *not a single time* did a sentence begin with a dependent clause or with a transitional word other than a pronoun. *Every* sentence began with the subject of an independent clause or that subject and a few modifying words.[3] To show you, I'll quote the first few words from every sentence (and I'll capitalize the subject and its word-modifiers):

From government writing:

> *This* amends . . .
> *These revisions* are . . .

From military writing:

> *There* are . . .[4]
> *Aircraft components and assemblies* are . . .
> *The latter* is . . .
> *Time-between-overhaul* is . . .
> *Airframe overhaul requirements* are . . .
> *Missile overhaul requirements* are . . .
> *Missile system end items* . . . are . . .

From business writing:

> *Growing businesses* must . . .
> *Such growth* . . . comes . . .
> *Buildings* can . . .
> *Proper planning* can . . .

From academic writing:

> *Psycholinguistic activity* is . . .
> *A major goal* . . . is . . .
> *The experiments* were . . .

See the problem? As I mentioned in Chapter 1, it as though the writer thinks of a sentence, writes it down, and stops; thinks of another sentence, writes it down, and stops; thinks of another sentence. . . . The writing is in sentences, one at a time, instead of in ideas. Naturally, then, there is little connection between the sentences, no thread tying one to another. The sentences exist, instead, as discrete chunks, as individual units that don't connect to each other. No wonder they're hard to read.

Now there's nothing wrong with beginning sentences with the subjects of independent clauses, but there is something wrong with beginning all sentences that way.

What can you do? There are many good ways to begin sentences (although the gobbledygook writers don't seem to find them): with prepositional phrases, with subordinate clauses, etc. Yet there are two beginnings—conjunctive adverbs and coordinating conjunctions—you might consider using more often, not for beginning every sentence, of course, but whenever they signal the right relationship.

Conjunctive Adverbs

Conjunctive adverbs are among the handiest devices for showing the relationship between one sentence and the next. In fact, another name for them is "sentence adverbs." Here are some common ones:

accordingly	furthermore	nevertheless
also	hence	next
anyway	however	on the other hand
as a result	incidentally	otherwise
besides	indeed	still
consequently	in fact	then
finally	instead	therefore
first (etc.)	likewise	thus
for example	meanwhile	unfortunately
for instance	moreover	

You can see that these words could be helpful in relating sentences. Here's an example:

Without Conjunctive Adverbs: Today's market for small automobiles is quite unstable. The major car manufacturers cannot predict how many cars they should produce.

With a Conjunctive Adverb: Today's market for small automobiles is quite unstable. *As a result,* the major car manufacturers cannot predict how many cars they should produce.

See how the conjunctive adverb shows the relationship between the two sentences?

You may say that you could understand the relationship perfectly well in the first case, the one without the conjunctive adverb. Of course. The sentences are short, the words are simple, and the ideas are easy. Still, I say that the example with the conjunctive adverb is easier for you to read. The reason? In the first example, you have to infer the relationship between the two sentences after reading both of them all the way through. Reading and making inferences, as I showed in the last chapter, requires more from your limited capacity processor, your brain, than does reading without making inferences.

Besides, the real question isn't so much why use them as it is why not. Some people think they know why not: conjunctive adverbs have the reputation of being heavy-handed, of being a sledge-hammer way of showing relationships. Perhaps our gobble-dygook writers in Chapter 1 had heard that argument. Maybe that is why they so industriously avoided using any of them to start their sentences. And you noticed how "light-handed" those writers were, their "delicate touch" with transitions, their "finesse" with words. . . .

Conjunctive adverbs are excellent words to show relationships. They work. People understand them easily. Use them with a clear conscience.

Coordinating Conjunctions

I gave you a long list of the conjunctive adverbs in the last section. In this section I'll cover another good transitional device: coordinating conjunctions. The list of them is much shorter:

and, but, or, nor, for, so, yet

Each word is short, and three of them rhyme with each other.

Perhaps you remember from grade school that you shouldn't ever begin sentences with words like "and." That may actually have been good advice then, for that stage of your development.[5] Children tend to string together all of their independent clauses with "and" words:

> I went to the store with Mary Ann and we bought some candy bars and then we put them in our pockets but when we tried to eat them they were all melted and sticky.

This immature sentence (for most contexts) doesn't begin with "and," but many of its independent clauses (which are prototypical sentences) do.

Children who write such sentences haven't yet learned to reduce some ideas to subordinate clauses or phrases. Here, then, is a more mature version:

> When I was at the store with Mary Ann, we bought some candy bars. We put them in our pockets, but when we tried to eat them they were melted and sticky.

The advice in grade school, then, to avoid beginning sentences with coordinating conjunctions may well be good. It helps stop students from overusing such words.

As a mature person, you are not likely to use coordinating conjunctions the way fourth graders do. Yet many times, as in this sentence, there are perfectly good times to use such words at the beginnings of sentences, appropriate times for the signal they carry. An alternative, of course, is simply to make the second sentence—the one that begins with a coordinating conjunction—a part of the first one by tacking it on, like this:

> As a mature person, you are not likely to use coordinating conjunctions the way fourth graders do, *yet* many times, as in this sentence, there are perfectly good times to use such words at the beginnings of sentences, appropriate times for the signal they carry.

The sentence is now rather long, isn't it—perhaps too long? Starting a new sentence with the coordinating conjunction "yet" solves that problem.

Starting sentences with coordinating conjunctions, then, is a good way to break up long sentences and still signal the relationship between the ideas. The alternative of writing a long sentence isn't always good; the alternative of writing two sentences and leaving out the transition isn't good; and the alternative of totally revising the two sentences just to avoid starting one of them with a coordinating conjunction doesn't make much sense.

Many good writers start sentences with coordinating conjunctions. If you check some writing you consider good—magazines you like, for instance—you will probably be surprised at how many professional writers use this technique frequently.

Subordinating Conjunctions

Whereas the conjunctions we just talked about—coordinating conjunctions—begin *independent* clauses, *su*bordinating conjunctions begin *dependent* clauses. There's really no controversy about using subordinating conjunctions; virtually all authorities recommend them heartily, as do I. They're important road signs.

Here are a few examples:

after	if	though
although	provided	unless
as if	provided that	until
as long as	since	when
as though	so that	where
because	than	while
before		whether

Although there is no controversy over the value of these words, ineffective writers often don't use them enough.

An ineffective writer, for example, might write sentences like these:

The law states clearly that property owners are responsible for accidents during non-working hours. Our company will not pay your hospital bill.

Now let's revise those sentences, showing the relationship between them by beginning with a subordinating conjunction:

> *Because* the law states clearly that property owners are responsible for accidents during non-working hours, our company will not pay your hospital bill.

Now the writer has made the reader's job a little easier. And imagine the difference between reading someone who habitually uses those road sign words and reading someone who habitually (sentence after sentence, page after page) leaves them out.

USE INFORMAL PUNCTUATION

Another good way to signal the relationships between sentences is to use two of the marks of punctuation normally associated with informal writing: the question mark and the dash. They are handy tools for a writer—tools that too often lie neglected in a dusty corner of the workshop.

Question Marks

About ten years ago, someone asked me if I could remember the last time I had used a question mark for anything other than personal letters. I hadn't used one for years.[6]

My mind was still cluttered with the proscription that someone, somewhere had made against rhetorical questions: Don't ever use them. So I didn't—or any other kind of question—but I still can't remember who told me that.[7]

A rhetorical question is one that seems to provide its own answer. Here are a few examples:

> Isn't our football team wonderful?

> Isn't our football team awful?

> Have you asked yourself recently when the last time was that you used a question mark?

Those questions seem to answer themselves.

Yet rhetorical questions and other kinds are important ways to signal relationships. When you read a question, you know that either an answer or an explanation will follow.

There is another, even better, reason to use questions: they engage your readers' attention, almost demand it. It's almost as though you are there, talking with them and expecting them to answer. Oftentimes, I think they do answer, too. I find myself paying special attention when I read a question, pausing briefly and mentally answering it.

I remember quite well when someone demonstrated the advantage of questions to me. Several of us were given about four hours to edit a two-hundred page, highly technical report. It was an investigation of a complex system having serious problems.

As you might guess, the report was almost unreadable. It was in gobbledygook, of course, and it was too technical for us, yet the intended audience was supposed to know no more about its technicalities than we did. The report was a classic case of a writer assuming that the reader knew everything he did.

In four hours, we naturally couldn't be much help, but we did try to improve the abstract, the short summary of the report that appeared at its beginning. The key sentence in the abstract—the one that said whether or not the system under investigation could be salvaged—was buried near the end of the abstract in the middle of a paragraph. It went something like this (I've changed the name of the system):

> An operationally effective and satisfactorily performing X-40 system is possible only if additional funding is made available to accommodate the requisite time for a more orderly completion of the system development effort.

I watched as one of my friends excavated that important sentence, put it in a paragraph by itself, and turned it into a question and an answer:

> Will the X-40 system work? Yes, but we'll have to spend more money to pay the contractor for the extra time he now needs.

See how the question draws attention to itself and the answer? See how smoothly those two sentences work together? You can almost visualize the reader seeing the first sentence, the question, and saying to himself, "Quick! Quick! What's the answer? I want to know!" That kind of question is sure to engage his attention.

Dashes

I think dashes have a bad reputation from the kinds of letters high school students are likely to write, letters with one dash after another. Yet just because dashes can be misused doesn't mean you shouldn't use them at all.

Arn Tibbetts, in an article in *The Journal of Business Communication*, shows that the dash is a good device for breaking a long sentence into more processible units. Consider this sentence:

> There have been no flu deaths from even the most virulent types of the disease for the past ten years in the country.[8]

Tibbetts then revised the sentence into smaller units—the kind our short-term memory can handle more easily:

> For the past ten years, there have been no flu deaths in the country—not even from the most virulent types of the disease.[9]

The dash, then, is a good way to break a sentence into good sizes for the short-term memory. But it also works as a road sign. In the example above, it means "and here's something else about the point I just made." That, in fact, is a common meaning for the dash.

However, you may wonder if Tibbetts couldn't simply have replaced the dash in the example above with a comma? In this case, probably so, although the dash seems to point with greater emphasis to what follows. Yet sometimes sentences can be in so many small units—which are good for processing—that a couple sets of commas can be confusing:

> If the larger trees, most of them evergreens, which provide year-round protection, but to some extent even leafy varieties, are planted on the north sides of the farm houses, then they will be helpful against the cold winter winds.

Now let's use dashes instead of one of the sets of commas:

If the larger trees, most of them evergreens—which provide
year-round protection—but to some extent even leafy varie-
ties, are planted on the north sides of the farm houses, then
they will be helpful against the cold winter winds.

See how the dashes help you keep track of where internal units begin and end?

Notes for Chapter 9

1.   John D. Bransford and Marcia K. Johnson, "Considerations of Some
Problems of Comprehension," in *Visual Information Processing*, ed. William G.
Chase (New York: Academic Press, 1973), p. 400.

2.   David E. Rumelhart, "Schemata: The Building Blocks of Cognition," in
Comprehension and Teaching: Research Reviews, ed. John T. Gutherie (Newark,
Del.: International Reading Association, 1981), 23.

3.   I do not wish to imply that none of these sentences has any form of
transition: The first two begin with demonstrative pronouns ("This" and "These"),
which clearly serve as ties to previous material; a later one begins with "Such," another tie to previous material.

Rather, my point is that these writers—typical, I believe of gobbledygook
writers—do not often use the key transitioning devices of conjunctive adverbs
and subordinating conjunctions. Also, they tend to think, and to write, in sentences, as indicated by their compulsion to begin sentences with independent
clauses instead of with words or phrases or clauses that tie one sentence or idea
with the previous one. That only three of the sixteen sentences from my samples
of bad writing begin with *any* kind of transition, and that all sixteen begin with the
subject of an independent clause or the few words that modify that subject, supports my assertion, I believe.

4.   I think for the purposes here, we can consider "there are" to be a
"dummy subject."

5.   Kellogg Hunt ran some studies on the syntactic abilities of students and
adults. He discusses the development of syntactic maturity, a disputed term in
the field of English these days, in his article "Early Blooming and Late Blooming
Syntactic Structures," in *Evaluating Writing*, ed. Charles R. Cooper and Lee Odell
(n.p.: National Council of Teachers of English, 1977), pp. 91-104.

Also, the example I give of "immature" sentence structure—stringing together words with "and" and "but"—really depends on the context. If the writer were trying to convey excitement, for instance, the example I give might well be an example of *mature* sentence structure. But my point in the chapter remains: children usually pass through a stage in which they overuse the coordinating conjunctions.

6.   In a study of writing by 17-year olds, Paul Diehl, Richard Lloyd-Jones, John Mellon, and Carl Klaus make a good point about question marks:

> [Good papers by the 17-year olds] also ask questions more often, more than twice as often as [the writers of weaker papers. Good writers] do not trap themselves in a strictly declarative mode of thinking but occasionally enter the role of one who seeks as well as gives information. Such a stance acknowledges not only that issues have more than one side but also that there is an audience to interact with, an interaction obvious in oral situations but too often forgotten in written ones. (*Correlation of Syntactic / Stylistic Fluency with Rhetorical Fluency and Judgment in the Persuasive Writing of 17-Year Olds*, p. 29)

I think that this insight—that writers who use questions have an essentially different relationship with their readers than writers who do not—is particularly valuable. In fact, you might test yourself: Do *you* use questions in *your* writing?

7.   One guess at the rationale against using rhetorical questions is that English teachers in the past (and some "traditionalists" today) had an aversion to "oral" writing, writing that used the techniques of speaking. Now, of course, many English teachers are trying to undo the damage of the past by urging people to write the way they talk.

8.   Arn Tibbetts, "Ten Rules for Writing *Readably*," *The Journal of Business Communication*, 18, No. 4 (1982), 55. Tibbetts misuses the term "chunking" in his article, but I like this example on the dash.

9.   Tibbetts, p. 55.

10 BE CAREFUL WITH YOUR SENTENCE STRUCTURE

You've probably heard that to write clearly, you should write short sentences. That's a commonplace in traditional books on clear writing. But like most commonplaces, this one needs a closer look.

Let's start with the concern over sentence length, and then look at two prominent types of long sentences—the cumulative and the periodic—to see how "readable" they are.

SHORT VERSUS LONG SENTENCES

Two of the best-known traditional books on clear writing emphasize that sentences—or average sentences—should be short. Robert Gunning, in *The Technique of Clear Writing*, makes it his "Principle 1."[1] Rudolf Flesch, in *On Business Communications*, devotes a chapter to it.[2] In fact, Flesch presents just the kind of argument for short sentences that I want to disagree with right now. Somehow he manages to be very right and very wrong at the same time:

> So the recipe for writing *really* short sentences (averaging well under 20 words) is to write every so often a very short sentence that says something crisply and decisively and then

> stops. To do that you have to be alert enough to hit the bull's-eye every few sentences or so. You can't go along in your usual fashion, answering your incoming letters one after another, stringing the same tired old phrases together, half asleep and utterly bored with your job. You've got to sit up straight, pull yourself together and pay attention.... Have a cup of strong coffee before you start. And then watch the average sentence length of your writing drop to 16 words, or 13, or 10.[3]

From 20 to 16 to 13 to 10? I wonder if getting to zero would be perfection?

Flesch is a word counter, and word counting is seldom helpful in determining readability. Besides, where does Flesch get 20 as some sort of magic number, anyway? (Breaking the "20-word barrier" he calls it elsewhere.)[4] Why *20* words instead of, say, 25 or 15?

Flesch also says that the key to having a low average sentence length is to throw in some really short sentences, saying something "crisply and decisively" and then stopping. (By the way, I think that too many people, for too long, have hidden behind terms like "crisp" and "decisive"—from Bishop Lowth's "solemn and elevated" to Strunk and White's "direct" and "bold."[5] Just what do these words mean? Do they mean any more, really, than Flesch's 20-word barrier?)

I don't think tossing in a few short sentences to decrease the average sentence length makes much sense. Presumably writing that has a high average sentence length is hard to read because it has a lot of long sentences. But if long sentences are hard to read, then how will an occasional short one make the longer ones any easier?

In fact, the "short" ones aren't always easy. Here's a sentence that would help keep average sentence length under the 20 words Flesch recommends. Yet I find it pretty tough going:

> A Center-directed committee review session report on the proceedings of the recently appointed board has been prepared.

So *short* sentences aren't necessarily *easy* to read.

And *long* sentences aren't necessarily *hard*. Here's a long one, much longer than Flesch's criterion of 20 words for average sentence length, yet I find it easy—if gruesome—reading. Tom Wolfe, the author, is telling us about a military wife who is about to learn that her husband was killed in a plane crash:

> When the final news came, there would be a ring at the front door—a wife in this situation finds herself staring at the front door as if she no longer owns it or controls it—and outside the door would be a man ... come to inform her that unfortunately something has happened out there, and her husband's body now lies incinerated in the swamps or the pines or the palmetto grass, "burned beyond recognition," which anyone who had been around an air base for very long (fortunately Jane had not) realized was quite an artful euphemism to describe a human body that now looked like an enormous fowl that has burned up in a stove, burned a blackish brown all over, greasy and blistered, fried, in a word, with not only the entire face and all the hair and the ears burned off, not to mention all the clothing, but also the *hands* and *feet*, with what remains of the arms and legs bent at the knees and elbows and burned into absolutely rigid angles, burned a greasy blackish brown like the bursting body itself, so that this husband, father, officer, gentleman, this *ornamentum* of some mother's eye, His Majesty the Baby of just twenty-odd years back, has been reduced to a charred hulk with wings and shanks sticking out of it.[6]

How many words? 223.

What, then, makes some sentences—short or long—hard or easy to read? I contend that the *structure* of a sentence is far more important than its length in determining readability. Let's turn to reading theory for the explanation.

The short-term memory has its limits, as we have seen. Certain kinds of long sentences don't exceed those limits: their structure lets the reader begin integrating their meaning into his long term memory as he reads them, instead of having to finish them before they make any sense. Usually sentences that are easy to read have the subject and the verb near the beginning, so the reader can gain early closure and a perspective on the rest of the sentence. I gave you an example of such an easy sentence in Chapter 7 ("We found out that pirates have ships, that ants have hills. . . .).

But sentences that are hard to read often have a structure that prevents the reader from making sense of them as he goes along. Perhaps they have too many words—especially abstract or low-frequency words—before the reader gets to the subject and verb. That asks the reader to hold too much in his short-term memory. Or perhaps a sentence has too many words *between* the subject and the verb, also overtaxing the short-term memory.

Here's an example of a sentence that's hard because it has too many words between the subject and the verb. It's from a Department of Defense regulation. See if your short-term memory overloads:

> The security classification *to be applied to information involved in User Agency contracts and programs* will be supplied by the contracting officer and his/her designated representative of the User Agency concerned.[7]

See what happens? You have to try to keep too many words in your short-term memory for too long. The only way to understand the sentence is to keep rereading it until you can build parts of it into "chunks."

Does sentence length, then, have *anything* to do with readability? Not if sentences have a good structure. But I'll certainly admit that sometimes bad writers could improve their writing by using shorter sentences. After all, we would prefer to read 15-word sentences with a bad structure than 25-word sentences with a bad one, wouldn't we? And sometimes, as we edit our writing, we find that we're better off using several sentences than one longer one. I certainly don't want to insist writing should be all in long sentences.

But if you read some of the best essayists, like E. B. White and George Orwell, you'll see that their sentences tend to be far longer than the sentences high school students, or even college students, typically produce.

But I have one more point to make. People who take Flesch's advice too seriously and try to cut their sentence length, often do it the wrong way. For example, suppose someone decided that the following sentence is too long.

Because today's market for small automobiles is quite unstable, the major car manufacturers cannot predict how many cars they should produce.

This would be an unfortunate sentence according to Flesch because it has 21 words. It helps push average sentence length over the 20-word barrier.

Writers who mistakenly try to reduce the size of such a sentence might simply divide it into two parts. But look what happens:

Today's market for small automobiles is quite unstable. The major car manufacturers cannot predict how many cars they should produce.

See the problem? Yes, we now have two sentences, one with 8 words and the other with 12—an average of only 10 words per sentence. But the problem is that those two sentences are now *harder* on the reader, not easier.

To change one sentence into two, what did we do? We left out the word "because," one of the road sign words we discussed in the last chapter, a signal for how the first part of the sentence relates to the second half. We now have two short sentences that are slightly harder to read than the one long one they came from.

Shorter, then, is not always better.

CUMULATIVE SENTENCES

For the rest of this chapter, let's look briefly at two special types of long sentences that style courses often teach, the cumulative sentence and the periodic sentence, and consider their "readability."

A cumulative sentence is one that usually begins with the subject and the verb of the independent clause and then adds modifiers afterwards—in other words, it *accumulates* modifiers. Here's a fairly simple example (I've underlined the subject and the verb of the independent clause):

We caught two bass, hauling them in briskly as though they were mackeral, pulling them over the side of the boat in a busi-

nesslike manner without any landing net, and stunning them
with a blow on the back of the head.[8] (E. B. White)

For a sentence to be cumulative, at least some of the modifiers
have to be "free modifiers," but let's not worry about definitions or
technicalities here. In practice, usually any modifier that can be
set off by commas counts.

A cumulative sentence, then, is one that starts with the subject and the verb—or at least has them close to the beginning of
the sentence—and then ends with some modifying words,
phrases, or clauses. Francis Christensen, who popularized the cumulative sentence, illustrated them by showing that they have different "levels." For example, here are the two levels in our sample
sentence by E. B. White:

1   We caught two bass,

  2   hauling them briskly as though they were mackeral,

  2   pulling them over the side of the boat in a businesslike
       manner without any landing net,

  2   and stunning them with a blow on the back of the
       head.

That sentence is fairly simple for a cumulative sentence. Here
are some other examples, not quite so simple:

I wait and *watch,* guarding the desert, the arches, the sand and
barren rock, the isolated junipers and scattered clumps of
sage surrounding me in stillness and simplicity under the
starlight.[9] (Edward Abbey)

The *mornings are* the pleasantest times in the apartment, ex-
haustion having set in, the sated mosquitoes at rest on ceiling
and walls, sleeping it off, the room a swirl of tortured bed-
clothes and abandoned garments, the vines in their full leafi-
ness filtering the hard light of day, the air conditioner silent at
last, like the mosquitoes.[10] (E. B. White)

The *San Bernardino Valley lies* only an hour east of Los Angeles
but *is* in certain ways an alien place: not the coastal California

of the subtropical twilights and the soft westerlies off the Pacific but a harsher California, haunted by the Mojave just beyond the mountains, devastated by the hot dry Santa Ana wind that comes down through the passes at 100 miles an hour and whines through the eucalyptus windbreaks and works on the nerves.[11] (Joan Didion)

With these excerpts, we have obviously stepped beyond only clear writing to literature. Just notice the poetry of the first excerpt and count the "s" sounds that make it beautiful to listen to. And read each excerpt aloud, listening for the prose rhythm, the beauty of the words not just in their sense but also in their sound.

Yet these passages are eminently readable, too, aren't they? They're long sentences, in most cases helping to demolish Flesch's "20-word barrier" for average sentence length, yet we can understand them the first time through. Why?

I explained in the last section that sentences with a good structure—such as having the subject and verb early and some sort of pattern that meets the reader's expectations—are the easiest to read. Cumulative sentences seem to be designed as easy reading: by definition the subject and verb come early and the following modifiers are in patterned segments, usually fairly short segments, set off by commas.

But I think there's another reason cumulative sentences are often easy to read. They seem to have a rhythm, caused by the segmentation. Just *listen* to them as you read them aloud. There's a rhythm to all of these sentences, a rhythm that carries you onward rather than holds you back.

These are sentences with sounds to them, important sounds. We think of the writer as "talking" to us, saying the words (remember the advice to "write the way you talk"?), and we think of ourselves as listeners.

Richard Lanham, in *Revising Prose*, also believes that prose rhythm is a valuable aid to readability:

[Bureaucratic sentences] just go on and on, as if they were emerging from a nonstop sausage machine. This shapelessness makes them unreadable: you cannot read them aloud with expressive emphasis. Try to. When language as spoken and heard has completely atrophied, the sentence becomes less a shaped unit of emphatic utterance than a shopping bag of words. Read your own prose aloud and with emphasis—or better still, have a friend read it to you.[12]

You might take Lanham's advice a step farther and try reading aloud some prose that you think is especially good, prose by notable writers, such as E. B. White, George Orwell, Joan Didion, Edward Abbey, Loren Eiseley, and Lewis Thomas. You will find there cumulative sentences, of course, and with them, compelling rhythm and remarkable clarity.

PERIODIC SENTENCES

Think of a periodic sentence as the opposite of a cumulative sentence in form: in a periodic sentence, the modifiers come first, then the subject and verb. Here's a sample:

> The wretched prisoners huddling in the stinking cages of the lock-ups, the grey, cowed faces of the long-term convicts, the scarred buttocks of the men who had been flogged with bamboos—all *these oppressed* me with an intolerable sense of guilt.[13] (George Orwell)

Periodic sentences set up patterns, but the pattern, unfortunately, comes before closure is likely, before the subject and the verb. Thus, a reader is unlikely to be able to integrate information from the short-term memory into the long-term memory. That's why people often have to reread periodic sentences. Perhaps you had to reread the excerpt above to understand it fully.

On the second reading, you can usually understand a periodic sentence easily, though, because you know what the subject and verb are, having just read them.

Still, periodic sentences aren't all bad. First, sometimes the context before a periodic sentence helps you enough so that you can understand it. Here's the Orwell sentence again, this time with the two preceding sentences:

> As for the job I was doing, I hated it more bitterly than I can perhaps make clear. In a job like that you see the dirty work of Empire at close quarters. *The wretched prisoners huddling in the stinking cages of the lock-ups, the grey, cowed faces of the long-term convicts, the scarred buttocks of the men who had*

been flogged with bamboos—all these oppressed me with an intolerable sense of guilt.

With the context, especially the words "the dirty work of Empire," you could perhaps make sense of the sentence the first time through.

A second reason not to ignore periodic sentences is that they are often so invested with rhythm that they draw special attention to themselves. In many cases, and in many kinds of writing, clarity is not the primary goal. Authors of literature are often involved with the sound as well as the meaning of their words. Periodic sentences can often contribute to an effective "sound."

As much as I enjoy writing and reading periodic sentences, I'm going to add a qualification. Authors who totally ignore readability are doing so at some peril, the peril of losing their readers. Good writing is worth the effort; bad writing is not. For practical writing that conducts day-to-day business, short periodic sentences—which don't overload the short-term memory before the closure with the subject and the verb—are usually fine. And an occasional long periodic sentence may be not only fun but also practical: it can attract and achieve emphasis. Use it for that purpose. But practical writing laden with periodic sentences will more likely frustrate rather than please the reader.

Notes for Chapter 10

1. Robert Gunning, *The Technique of Clear Writing*, revised ed. (New York: McGraw-Hill, 1968), pp. 49-64.

2. Rudolf Flesch, *On Business Communications* (New York: Barnes and Noble, 1972), p. 64. I know I am rough on Flesch here, even though he is saying only what many others were saying at the time. So I'll again protest that the book is the best of the bunch and still worth reading.

3. Flesch, p. 64.

4. Flesch, p. 64.

5. In commenting on Strunk and White's use of such terms, Monroe Beardsley asks these questions: What if we don't feel bold and decisive (we want a favor from someone)? What if we don't want to appear that way? [From "Style and Good Style," in *Contemporary Essays on Style*, ed. Glen A. Love and Michael Payne (Glenview, Ill.: Scott, Foresman, 1969), p. 8.]

6.   Tom Wolfe, *The Right Stuff* (New York: Bantam, 1979), p. 3.

7.   Department of Defense Manual 5220.22-M, p. 41.

8.   E. B. White, "Once More to the Lake," in *The Essays of E. B. White* (New York: Harper and Row, 1977), p. 199.

9.   Edward Abbey, "Solitaire," in *Desert Solitaire* (New York: Ballantine Books, 1968), p. 14.

10.   E. B. White, "Will Strunk," in *Essays of E. B. White* (New York: Harper and Row, 1977), p. 257.

11.   Joan Didion, "Some Dreamers of the Golden Dream," in *Slouching towards Bethlehem* (New York: Washington Square Press, 1968), p. 19.

12.   Richard Lanham, *Revising Prose* (New York: Charles Scribner's Sons, 1979), p. 9.

13.   George Orwell, "Shooting an Elephant," in *A Collection of Essays by George Orwell* (New York: Harcourt Brace Jovanovich, 1953), p. 148.

11   A LAST WORD

I'll close with a quotation from William Hazlitt, a renowned British writer of the early nineteenth century. This is from the beginning of his famous essay, "On Familiar Style":

> It is not easy to write a familiar style.... There is nothing that requires more precision, and, if I may say so, purity of expression, than the style I am speaking of.[1]

That's a good quotation for the last chapter—first person, easy words, and a preposition at the end.

Is Hazlitt right, though? Is writing in a familiar style—that is, writing informally—difficult to do? It's certainly harder than watching baseball on a Saturday afternoon. In a way, it may even be harder than writing gobbledygook, too. Writing gobbledygook is slipshod. It doesn't demand much in the way of Hazlitt's "precision" or "purity of expression." It can be sloppy, literally thoughtless, and nobody would know the difference.

Yet most gobbledygook writers don't write thoughtlessly. They try hard, and writing for them—even to get their murky ideas down in murkier words—is a terrible struggle, a nightmare, a frustrating and hopeless ordeal. And, unfortunately, the result doesn't repay the effort.

Once you learn to write the way you talk, once you have the breakthrough I did while writing my first book, the struggle, the nightmare, the ordeal will end. You will feel that *you* are in command, not the writing.

You will still have to work hard to be precise, and, as I discussed in Chapter 3, you will have to work hard even to understand what you mean, since writing is almost always a process of discovery. Yet that process will be a far easier one for you to go through than the frustrating and sterile process of the gobbledygook writer. And not just the process, but the results—the words and ideas you put on paper—will be more rewarding.

Note for Chapter 11

1. William Hazlitt, "On Familiar Style," from *Selected Essays of William Hazlitt*, ed. Geoffrey Keynes (New York: Random House, 1948), p. 474.

BIBLIOGRAPHY

Books

Adelstein, Michael A. *Contemporary Business Writing*. New York: Random House, 1971.

Andrews, Clarence A. *Technical and Business Writing*. Boston: Houghton Mifflin, 1975.

Barzun, Jacques. *On Writing, Editing, and Publishing*. Chicago: University of Chicago Press, 1971.

──────. *Simple & Direct: A Rhetoric for Writers*. New York: Harper and Row, 1976.

Britton, James. *Language and Learning*. Coral Gables, Florida: University of Miami Press, 1970.

Britton, James, et al. *The Development of Writing Abilities* (11-18). London: MacMillen, 1975.

Dale, Edgar, and Jeanne S. Chall. *A Formula for Predicting Readability*. Columbus, Ohio: Ohio State University, n.d.

Elbow, Peter. *Writing without Teachers*. London: Oxford University Press, 1973.

Emig, Janet. *The Composing Process of Twelfth Graders*. Urbana, Ill.: National Council of Teachers of English, 1971.

Felker, Daniel B., et al. *Guidelines for Document Designers*. Washington, D. C.: American Institutes for Research, n.d.

Flesch, Rudolf. *The Art of Plain Talk.* New York: Harper and Brothers, 1946.

—————. *The Art of Readable Writing.* New York: Collier, 1949.

—————. *On Business Communications.* New York: Barnes and Noble, 1972.

Flower, Linda. *Problem-Solving Strategies for Writing.* New York: Harcourt Brace Jovanovich, 1981.

Foss, Donald J., and David T. Hakes. *Psycholinguistics: An Introduction to the Psychology of Language.* Englewood Cliffs, N.J.: Prentice-Hall, 1978.

Fowler, H. W. *A Dictionary of Modern English Usage.* London: Oxford University Press, 1926.

Freedle, Roy O., ed. *New Directions in Discourse Processing.* Vol. 2. Norwood, N.J.: Ablex, 1979.

Gibson, Walker. *The Limits of Language.* New York: Hill and Wang, 1962.

—————. *Persona: A Style Guide for Readers and Writers.* New York: Random House, 1969.

Gibson, Walker. *Tough, Sweet & Stuffy.* Bloomington, Indiana: Indiana University Press, 1966.

Glucksberg, Sam, and Joseph H. Danks. *Experimental Psycholinguistics: An Introduction.* New York: Lawrence Erlbaum Associates, 1975.

Graves, Robert, and Alan Hodge. *The Reader over Your Shoulder.* 2nd ed. New York: Random House, 1971.

Gunning, Robert. *The Technique of Clear Writing.* Rev. ed. New York: McGraw-Hill, 1968.

Guthrie, John T., ed. *Comprehension and Teaching: Research Reviews.* Newark, Del.: International Reading Association, 1981.

Hairston, Maxine. *A Contemporary Rhetoric.* 2nd ed. Boston: Houghton Mifflin, 1978.

Halliday, M. A. K., and Ruqaiya Hasan. *Cohesion in English.* London: Longman, 1976.

Hirsch, E. D. *The Philosophy of Composition.* Chicago: University of Chicago Press, 1977.

Hoffman, Richard L., ed. *History of the English Language: Selected Texts and Exercises.* Boston: Little, Brown, 1968.

Holmes, Oliver Wendell. *The Common Law 3.* In *The Language of the Law* by David Mellinkoff. Boston: Little, Brown, 1963.

Irmscher, William F. *Teaching Expository Writing.* New York: Holt, Rinehart and Winston, 1979.

Kucera, Henry, and W. Nelson Francis. *Computational Analysis of Present-Day American English.* Providence, R. I.: Brown University Press, 1967.

Kuhn, Thomas. *The Structure of Scientific Revolutions.* 2nd ed., enlarged. Chicago: University of Chicago Press, 1970.

Lanham, Richard. *Revising Prose.* New York: Scribner's, 1979.

————. *Style: An Anti-Textbook.* New Haven: Yale University Press, 1974.

LaBerge, David, and S. Jay Samuels, ed. *Basic Processes in Reading: Perception and Comprehension.* Hillsdale, N.J.: Lawrence Erlbaum, 1977.

Lowth, Robert. *A Short Introduction to English Grammar.* Delmar, N.Y.: Scholars' Facsimiles & Reprints, 1979.

Macrorie, Ken. *Uptaught.* Rochelle Park, N.J.: Hayden, 1970.

Martin, Nancy, et al. *Writing and Learning across the Curriculum 11-16.* Schools Council Writing across the Curriculum Project, University of London Institute of Education. London: Hollen Street Press, 1976.

Mellinkoff, David. *The Language of the Law.* Boston: Little, Brown, 1963.

————. *Legal Writing: Sense and Nonsense.* St. Paul, Minnesota: West, 1982.

Mitchell, Richard. *Less than Words Can Say.* Boston: Little, Brown, 1979.

Murphy, Herta, and Charles E. Peck. *Effective Business Communication.* 3rd ed. New York: McGraw-Hill, 1980.

Newman, Edwin. *Strictly Speaking: Will America Be the Death of English?* New York: Warner Books, 1974.

O'Hayre, John. *Gobbledygook Has Gotta Go.* U.S. Department of the Interior, Bureau of Land Management. Washington, D.C.: GPO, n.d.

Quinn, Jim. *American Tongue in Cheek: A Populist Guide to Our Language.* New York: Penguin, 1980.

Read, Herbert. *English Prose Style.* New York: Pantheon, 1952.

Safire, William. *On Language.* New York: Times Books, 1980.

Shaughnessy, Mina P. *Errors and Expectations: A Guide for the Teacher of Basic Writing.* New York: Oxford, 1977.

Slobin, Dan Isaac. *Psycholinguistics.* 2nd ed. Glenview, Ill.: Scott, Foresman, 1979.

Smith, Frank. *Understanding Reading: A Psycholinguistic Analysis of Reading and Learning to Read.* 2nd ed. New York: Holt, Rinehart and Winston, 1978.

Stageberg, Norman. *Introductory English Grammar.* New York: Holt, Rinehart and Winston, 1965.

Strunk, William, Jr., and E. B. White. *The Elements of Style.* 3rd ed. New York: Macmillan, 1979.

Trimble, John R. *Writing with Style: Conversations on the Art of Writing.* Englewood Cliffs, N.J.: Prentice-Hall, 1975.

Vygotsky, Lev. *Thought and Language.* Trans. and ed. Eugenia Hanfmann and Gertrude Vakar. Cambridge, Mass.: The M.I.T. Press, 1962.

Wallas, Graham. *The Art of Thought.* New York: Harcourt, Brace, 1926. Selection quoted in *The Composing Process of Twelfth Graders* by Janet Emig. NCTE Research Report No. 13. Urbana, Ill.: National Council of Teachers of English, 1971, p. 17.

Williams, Joseph M. *Style: Ten Lessons in Clarity and Grace.* Glenview, Ill.: Scott, Foresman, 1981.

Wittgenstein, Ludwig. Aphorism quoted in *Style: Ten Lessons in Clarity and Grace* by Joseph Williams. Glenview, Ill.: Scott, Foresman, 1981), p. 1.

Zinsser, William. *On Writing Well.* New York: Harper and Row, 1976.

Articles

Adams, Marilyn Jager, and Allan Collins. "A Schema-Theoretic View of Reading." In *New Directions in Discourse Processing*, Vol. 2. Ed. Roy O. Freedle. Norwood, N. J.: Ablex, 1979, pp. 1-22.

Advertisement for Morton Buildings. *Business and Industry Magazine*, April 1982, p. 26.

Anderson, Richard C., and Peter Freebody. "Vocabulary Knowledge." In *Reading and Comprehension*. Ed. John T. Guthrie. Newark, Del.: International Reading Association, 1982, pp. 77-117.

Beardsley, Monroe. "Style and Good Style." In *Contemporary Essays on Style*. Ed. Glen A. Love and Michael Payne. Glenview, Ill.: Scott, Foresman, 1969, pp. 3-15.

Belmore, Susan M. "Drawing Inferences from Concrete and Abstract Sentences." *Journal of Verbal Learning and Verbal Behavior*, 21 (1982), 338-51.

Bransford, John D., and Marcia K. Johnson. "Considerations of Some Problems of Comprehension." In *Visual Information Processing*. Ed. William G. Chase. New York: Academic Press, 1973, pp. 383-438.

Broughton, Philip. "How to Win at Wordsmanship" (box insert). *Newsweek*, May 6, 1968, p. 104.

Cairns, Helen S., and Donald J. Foss. "Falsification of the Hypothesis That Word Frequency Is a Unified Variable in Sentence Processing." *Journal of Verbal Learning and Verbal Behavior*, 10 (1971), 41-43.

Cairns, Helen S., and Joan Kamerman. "Lexical Information Processing During Sentence Comprehension." *Journal of Verbal Learning and Verbal Behavior*, 14 (1975), 170-79.

Carpenter, Patricia A., and Meredyth Daneman. "Lexical Retrieval and Error Recovery in Reading: A Model Based on Eye Fixations." *Journal of Verbal Learning and Verbal Behavior*, 20 (1981), 137-60.

Carroll, John B., and Margaret N. White. "Age-of-Acquisition Norms for 220 Picturable Nouns." *Journal of Verbal Learning and Verbal Behavior*, 12 (1973), 563-76.

Cirilo, Randolph K. "Referential Coherence and Text Structure in Story Comprehension." *Journal of Verbal Learning and Verbal Behavior*, 20 (1981), 358-67.

Coleman, E. B. "The Comprehensibility of Several Grammatical Transformations." *Journal of Applied Psychology*, 48, No. 3 (1964), 186-90.

—————. "Learning of Prose Written in Four Grammatical Transformations." *Journal of Applied Psychology*, 49, No. 5 (1965), 332-41.

Cooper, Charles R. "Holistic Evaluation of Writing." In *Evaluating Writing.* Ed. Charles Cooper and Lee Odell. N.p.: NCTE, 1977.

Diehl, Paul, Richard Lloyd-Jones, John Mellon, and Carl Klaus. *Correlation of Syntactic / Stylistic Fluency and Judgment with Rhetorical Fluency and Judgment in the Persuasive Writing of 17-Year Olds.*

DiGaetani, John Louis. "Conversation: The Key to Better Business Writing." *Wall Street Journal*, February 8, 1982.

Dixon, Peter, and Ernst Z. Rothkopf. "Word Repetition, Lexical Access, and the Process of Searching Words and Sentences." *Journal of Verbal Learning and Verbal Behavior*, 18 (1979), 629-44.

Doherty, Paul C. "Hirsch's *Philosophy of Composition:* An Evaluation of the Argument." *College Composition and Communication*, 33, No. 2 (1982), 184-95.

Dooling, D. James, and Roy Lachman. "Effects of Comprehension on Retention of Prose." *Journal of Experimental Psychology*, 88, No. 2 (1971), 216-22.

Flower, Linda, and John R. Hayes. "A Cognitive Process Theory of Writing." *College Composition and Communication*, 32, No. 4 (1981), 365-87.

—————. "The Cognition of Discovery: Defining a Rhetorical Problem." *College Composition and Communication*, 31, No. 1 (1980), 21-32.

—————. "The Dynamics of Composing: Making Plans and Juggling Constraints." In *Cognitive Processes in Writing.* Ed. Lee W. Gregg and Erwin R. Steinberg. Hillsdale, N.J.: Lawrence Erlbaum Associates, 1980, pp. 31-50.

46 CFR Part 510. "Licensing of Independent Ocean Freight Forwarders." Federal Maritime Commission. *Federal Register* ("Rules and Regulations"), 47, No. 109 (June 7, 1982), 24555.

Foss, Donald J. "Decision Processes during Sentence Comprehension: Effects of Lexical Item Difficulty and Position upon Decision Times." *Journal of Verbal Learning and Verbal Behavior*, 8 (1969), 457-62.

—————. "Some Effects of Ambiguity upon Sentence Comprehension." *Journal of Verbal Learning and Verbal Behavior*, 9 (1970), 699-706.

Glanzer, Murray, and S. L. Ehrenreich. "Structure and Search of the Internal Lexicon." *Journal of Verbal Learning and Verbal Behavior*, 18 (1979), 381-98.

Glucksberg, Sam, Tom Trabasso, and Jerry Wald. "Linguistic Structures and Mental Operations." *Cognitive Psychology*, 5 (1973), 338-70.

Goldman, Susan R., et al. "Short-Term Retention of Discourse During Reading." *Journal of Educational Psychology*, 72, No. 5 (1980), 647-55.

Graesser, Arthur, Nicholas L. Hoffman, and Leslie F. Clark. "Structural Components of Reading Time." *Journal of Verbal Learning and Verbal Behavior*, 19 (1980), 135-51.

Hake, Rosemary, and Joseph M. Williams. "Style and Its Consequences: Do as I Do, Not as I Say." *College English*, 43, No. 5 (1981), 433-51.

Haviland, Susan E., and Herbert H. Clark. "What's New? Acquiring New Information as a Process in Comprehension." *Journal of Verbal Learning and Verbal Behavior,* 13 (1974), 512-21.

Hayes, John R. and Linda S. Flower. "Identifying the Organization of Writing Processes." In *Cognitive Processes in Writing.* Ed. Lee W. Gregg and Erwin R. Steinberg. Hillsdale, N.J.: Lawrence Erlbaum Associates, 1980.

Hazlitt, William. "On Familiar Style." In *Selected Essays of William Hazlitt.* Ed. Geoffrey Keynes. New York: Random House, 1948, pp. 474-82.

Hunt, Kellogg. "Early Blooming and Late Blooming Syntactic Strucures." In *Evaluating Writing.* Ed. Charles R. Cooper and Lee Odell. N.p.: NCTE, 1977, pp. 91-104.

Just, Marcel Adam, and Patricia A. Carpenter. "A Theory of Reading: From Eye Fixations to Comprehension." *Psychological Review,* 87, No. 4 (1980), 329-54.

Kester, John. "How to Speak Pentagonese: Translations from the Five-Sided World of the Military." *The Washingtonian,* February 1982, pp. 69-75.

Kintsch, Walter. "Toward a Model of Text Comprehension and Production." *Psychological Review,* 85, No. 5 (1978), 363-93.

Kintsch, W., and D. Monk. "Storage of Complex Information in Memory: Some Implications of the Speed with Which Interferences [sic: "Inferences"] Can Be Made." *Journal of Experimental Psychology,* 94, No. 1 (1972), 25-32.

Klare, George. "Assessing Readability." *Reading Research Quarterly,* 10, No. 1 (1974-75), 62-102.

LaBerge, David, and S. Jay Samuels. "Toward a Theory of Automatic Information Processing in Reading." *Cognitive Psychology,* 6 (1974), 293-323.

Levey, Bob. "Bob Levey's Washington." *The Washington Post,* September 6, 1982, p. D17.

Marks, Carolyn B., Marleen J. Doctorow, and M. C. Wittrock. "Word Frequency and Reading Comprehension." *The Journal of Educational Research,* 67, No. 6 (1974), 259-62.

Miller, George A., "The Magical Number Seven, Plus or Minus Two: Some Limits on Our Capacity for Processing Information." *The Psychological Review,* 63, No. 2 (1956), 81-97.

Mitchell, D. C., and D. W. Green. "The Effects of Context and Content on Immediate Processing in Reading." *Quarterly Journal of Experimental Psychology,* 30 (1978), 609-36.

Olson, Gary A. "Incorporating Sentence Combining into the Advanced Composition Class." *Journal of Advanced Composition,* 2, Nos. 1 & 2 (1981), 119-26.

Olson, David R., and Nikola Filby. "On the Comprehension of Active and Passive Sentences." *Cognitive Psychology,* 3 (1972), 361-81.

Paivio, Allan, John C. Yuille, and Stephen A. Madigan. "Concreteness, Imagery, and Meaningfulness Values for 925 Nouns." *Journal of Experimental Psychology Monograph Supplement,* 76, No. 1, Part 2 (1968), 1-25.

Paivio, Allan, and Kalman Csapo. "Picture Superiority in Free Recall: Imagery or Dual Coding?" *Cognitive Psychology*, 5 (1973), 176-206.

Pearson, P. David. "The Effects of Grammatical Complexity on Children's Comprehension, Recall, and Conception of Certain Semantic Relations." *Reading Research Quarterly*, 10, No. 2 (1974-75), 155-92.

Pearson, P. David, and Kaybeth Camperell. "Comprehension of Text Structures." In *Comprehension and Teaching*. Ed. John T. Guthrie. Newark, Del.: International Reading Association, 1982, pp. 27-55.

Petrosky, Anthony. "Review of *Problem-Solving Strategies for Writing*, Linda Flower." *College Composition and Communication*, 34, No. 2 (1983), 233-35.

Pierstorff, Don K. "Response to Linda Flower and John Hayes, 'A Cognitive Process Theory of Writing.'" *College Composition and Communication*, 34, No. 2 (1983), 217.

Rubenstein, Herbert, Lonnie Garfield, and Jane A. Millikan. "Homographic Entries in the Internal Lexicon." *Journal of Verbal Learning and Verbal Behavior*, 9 (1970), 487-94.

Rumelhart, David E. "Schemata: The Building Blocks of Cognition." In *Comprehension and Teaching*. Ed. John T. Guthrie. Newark, Del.: International Reading Association, 1981, pp. 3-26.

Sachs, Jacqueline Strunk. "Recognition Memory for Syntactic and Semantic Aspects of Connected Discourse." *Perception & Psychophysics*, 2, No. 9 (1967), 437-42.

Scarborough, Don L., Charles Cortese, and Hollis S. Scarborough. "Frequency and Repetition Effects in Lexical Memory." *Journal of Experimental Psychology: Human Perception and Performance*, 3, No. 1 (1977), 1-17.

Selzer, Jack. "Readability Is a Four-Letter Word." *The Journal of Business Communication*, 18, No. 4 (1982), 23-33.

Sledd, James. "The Lexicographer's Uneasy Chair." *College English*, 23, No. 8 (1962), 682-87.

Slobin, Dan I. "Grammatical Transformations and Sentence Comprehension in Childhood and Adulthood." *Journal of Verbal Learning and Verbal Behavior*, 5 (1966), 219-27.

Sommers, Nancy. "Response to Sharon Crowley, 'Components of the Process.'" *College Composition and Communication*, 29, No. 2 (1978), 209-11.

——————. "Revision Strategies of Student Writers and Experienced Adult Writers." *College Composition and Communication*, 31, No. 4 (1980), 378-88.

Stanovich, Keith E. "Toward an Interactive-Compensatory Model of Individual Differences in the Development of Reading Fluency." *Reading Research Quarterly*, 16, No. 1 (1980), 32-71.

Tibbetts, Arn. "Ten Rules for Writing Readably." *The Journal of Business Communication*, 18, No. 4 (1982), 53-62.

U.S. Congress. House Appropriations Committee. *DOD Appropriations for 1978: Part I, Budget Hearings,* 95th Congress. Washington, D.C.: GPO, 1977, pp. 277-78.

Vipond, Douglas. "Micro- and Macroprocesses in Text Comprehension." *Journal of Verbal Learning and Verbal Behavior,* 19 (1980), 276-96.

Williams, Joseph M. "Defining Complexity." *College English,* 40, No. 6 (1979), 595-609.

——————. "The Phenomenology of Error." *College Composition and Communication,* 32 (May 1981), 152-68.

Acknowledgments continued from copyright page:

John Louis DiGaetani, "Conversation: The Key to Better Business Writing," *Wall Street Journal,* Feb. 8, 1982, p. 26. Reprinted by permission of the author and *The Wall Street Journal,* © Dow Jones & Company, Inc., 1982. All rights reserved.

Marcel A. Just and Patricia A. Carpenter, "A Theory of Reading," *Psychological Review,* 87, No. 4 (July 1980), 330. Reprinted by permission of the authors.

Douglas Vipond, "Micro- and Macroprocesses in Text Composition," *Journal of Verbal Learning and Verbal Behavior,* 19 (1980), 291. Reprinted by permission of Academic Press, Inc.

Herta A. Murphy and Charles E. Peck, *Effective Business Communications,* 3rd ed., p. 49. Reprinted by permission of McGraw-Hill, Inc.

INDEX